The Elements of Cure

Cure:
To resolve an illness
by addressing cause
and consequences.

Illness:
In this text, an illness
Refers to a
curable illness.

Copyright: Tracy D Kolenchuk, 2019
- - - All Rights Reserved - - -

ISBN: 9781792968105

Dedication:

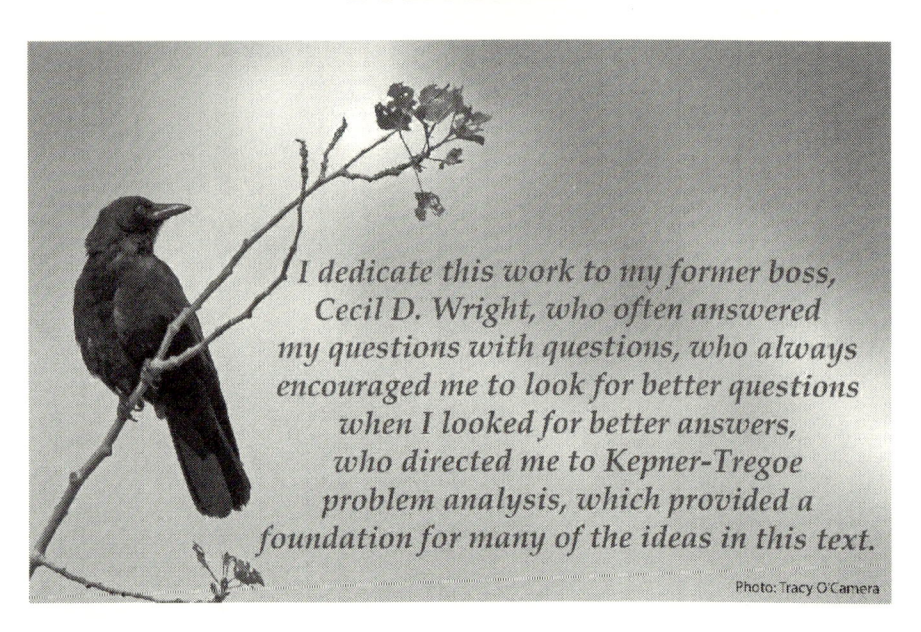

I dedicate this work to my former boss, Cecil D. Wright, who often answered my questions with questions, who always encouraged me to look for better questions when I looked for better answers, who directed me to Kepner-Tregoe problem analysis, which provided a foundation for many of the ideas in this text.

Photo: Tracy O'Camera

In the following quotes from Kepner-Tregoe's The Rational Manager (KT-TRM) and The New Rational Manager (KT-TNRM), I have added *illness* and *cure* in {} to show how Kepner-Tregoe can be related to curing.

"Problem solving {curing} requires cause and effect thinking" (KT-TNRM)

"A problem {illness} is the visible effect of a cause" "If performance {healthiness} once met the SHOULD and no longer does, then a change has occurred." "In some cases, however, a negative deviation in performance {an illness}... has always existed" (KT-TNRM)

The search for the cause of any problem {illness} ... is a search for the change, for the thing which is new, different, or unplanned, that upset {healthiness} (KT-TRM)

Preface: An Introduction to Healthiness

Sometimes the critical change that caused the problem {illness} may be so subtle or gradual that nobody is aware of it. (KT-TRM)

An improvement... for example, is frequently overlooked as a "change". (KT-TRM)

In some cases, problems {illnesses} will be interconnected through a chain of cause and effect... Thus the cause in turn becomes a new problem {illness} to be analyzed and explained, and its cause may in turn become yet another problem {illness} for study and solution {cure}. (KT-TRM)

"It is tempting to combine two or more deviations {illnesses} in a single problem-solving {curing} effort... This procedure is almost always inefficient and unproductive." (KT-TNRM)

"To verify a likely cause is to prove that it did produce the effect {the illness}. (KT-TNRM)

"Sometimes we take an action that just happens to correct {cure} the effect {the illness}, although the cause is never fully explained... At other times the cause is neither discovered nor stumbled upon, and no action corrects {cures} the effect. An interim, or holding, action must be devised so that the operation {patient} can live with the problem until its true cause is found" (KT-TNRM)

The entire Kepner-Tregoe methodology, developed in the 1960s has been taught to thousands of businessmen worldwide and has proven to be very successful in solving many types of problems. I believe it can be just as effective applied to health and medical problems.

Preface

There are few theories of medicine and only a single theory of cure in medicine today. Historical theories are many, from Hippocrates' humoral theory and Chinese medicine's theory of balancing yin and yang, to Ayurveda's attribution of health and disease to a complex set of balances and imbalances. Conventional medicine has the germ theory, woefully inadequate, even for many diseases caused by infectious agents. There are statistics about nutritional, genetic, and environmental causes of disease, without any general theories of cause. Words like health, illness, disease, disorder, disability and cure are not defined medically and not used consistently. Scientific definitions of these words do not exist.

> *The beginning of wisdom is the definition of terms.*
> *-- SOCRATES*

Medicine is a practice without a theory. This observation has been made by many philosophers, teachers, and students. Conventional medicine barely has a language of medicine – perhaps because there is no theory. Or, perhaps there is no theory because there is no language.

Cure, cures, curing, and cured are not defined in today's sciences of medicine. Many medical dictionaries do not define the word cure. No medical reference contains a scientific definition of cure. I have not seen a single medical reference to cure using the word **cause**. Medical texts use the word **treatment** ten times as often as **cure**. Many uses of cure in current medical references is **incurable** or a variation thereof.

Many cases of disease are diagnosed and treated without analysis of cause. Treatments for signs and symptoms are designed, tested, approved by governments, manufactured, recommended, and sold without intention to cure. The latest medical fashions of Science-Based Medicine and Functional Medicine also remain ignorant of the fundamental nature of causes of disease.

Conventional medicine is bureaucratic. Bureaucrats don't judge individual cases. They judge **by the book**. The books of medicine are cure deficient. Every cure is an individual case.

The Elements of Cure is a condensation, expansion, and update of the concepts explored in the book A Calculus of Curing – developed over several years of research and writing for the blog site Healthicine – the Arts and Sciences of Health and Healthiness. It is also an expansion of the paper A Definition and Exploration of Cure published on Academia.edu in July 2018. This book defines fundamental concepts of cure, cures, curing, and cured, and many related topics including cause, illness, disease, sickness, treatment, cured, and remission.

The Elements of Cure is based on theory and concepts health, and healthiness, of healthicine. These concepts are not necessary to understand the elements of cure, but a basic understanding provides a useful framework. Let's begin.

Health is Whole

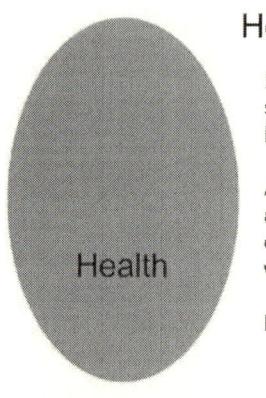

Health is whole.

Life is whole. We study health of individual life entities.

A person missing a tooth, or an arm, or a leg is still a whole person.

Health is always whole.

© Healthicine

We often say *"health is whole,"* but the concept is poorly studied.

Wholeness often refers to completeness to perfection. Health is whole, but never perfect, never complete. We must always strive for health until we die. But we must know we will die.

A Healthiness is a Measurable Unit of Health

Healthiness

A healthiness is a measurable unit of health, consisting of healthiness and unhealthiness.

Together, healthiness plus unhealthiness is 100 precent. A whole.

© Healthicine

The word *healthiness* hardly exists in medicine.

An illness is an instance of ill, of disease: observable, possibly diagnosable, measurable, treatable, curable.

A healthiness is a measurable instance of health.

Medicine has no concept of a healthiness, much less any techniques to measure individual instances of healthiness.

An unhealthiness is a potential for improvement in a specific dimension of healthiness. The wholeness of a healthiness consists of the current level of healthiness, and its corresponding level of unhealthiness.

An Illness is Hole in Health

An illness is a hole in health

Illnesses can appear when an unhealthiness grows too large, when healthiness shrinks, or from external causes.

Health is still whole.

© Healthicine

Health is not the opposite of illness; any more than earth is the opposite of a hole in the ground.

An illness is not the opposite of health, nor the opposite of a healthiness.

An illness is a hole in health.

Every illness has a Cause

Historical theories of medicine offer many different ideas about causes of illness and disease. Without realizing it, they also provide the fundamental underlying theory: *every illness has a cause*.

Every Cause is a Change

Every cause is a change. Every illness is caused by a change. Live things change, their environments change, they change their environments. Cause, changes are the starting points to an understanding of cure. There are two important types of cause, from a perspective of time. Injury illnesses have causes in the past, are a result of changes in the past. Non-injury illnesses have ongoing present causes, causing the illness, which are a result of a change, a cause in the past. Addressing past causes is useful for prevention, but seldom useful to cure. Change can cause illness, and only change can cure.

The change that causes or cures an illness might be in body, mind, spirits, or community. Even a change in belief, or perspective might cause, or cure an illness.

Every Cure has a Cause

Cures of injury illnesses come from healing. Cures of non-injury illnesses come from addressing present causes. When the cause is in the body, a physical change is required. When the cause is in the mind, a mental change is required. When the cause is in the spirit, a spirit change is required. When the cause is in the environment, an environmental change is required.

Preface: An Introduction to Healthiness

Examples Used in This Book

I have intentionally used simple examples in this text. Elementary cures are simple, by definition. I often use scurvy, a trivial disease in theory, although no current medical reference offers a cure, and it can become complex, chronic, difficult to cure, even deadly. My purpose is not to understand any individual patient's complex situation, rather to provide tools to deconstruct complex situations such that illnesses might be cured, and we might know they have been cured. As we begin to understand and use concepts of the elements of cure, every cause and every illness can be simplified. We must simplify to cure.

Who am I?

I am not a doctor nor a medical professional. I have no university degrees. I am a retired computer analyst, a student of system and technical problems. I am also the creator and a student of healthicine, the arts and sciences of health and healthiness.

We will cure more illnesses with health than with medicines.

A few years ago, I learned the word *cure* is not defined in many medical dictionaries. I began my quest to understand cure. Research via the internet took me back hundreds of years. The local university library archives contained historical medical texts not available online. Gradually, over the course of three years now, I wrote and rewrote, edited and re-edited, challenging my ideas again and again.

I learned a lot about curing and published the book: A Calculus of Curing. As I wrote, I recognized the need for a concise guide to the concepts of cure. This book is a summary. If you want more details, rationalization and discussion, consult A Calculus of Curing, although many concepts have been developed further in this text.

Health is whole.
Health is wide and deep.
Health is slow and steady.
Health is honest and true.
Health is the best preventative.
Health is the best cure, the only true cure.
*-- **The Healthicine Creed***

Webster's New World Medical Dictionary does not contain the words cure, cured, cures, nor incurable, nor does The Oxford Concise Medical Dictionary, Ninth Edition, 2015, nor The Bantam Medical Dictionary, Sixth Edition, 2009

It's time to put CURE back into the dictionaries.

Photo: Tracy O'Camera

Table of Contents

The Meanings of Cure 1

Illness 5

Causes of Illness 17

Causal Chains 23

Deficiencies or Excesses? 29

Consequences of Illness 33

Cure 37

Circles of Illness, Cause, Cure 59

Curing Causal Illness 65

Curing Injury Illness 67

Curing Attribute Illness 75

Illness, Injury, or Disability? 83

Curing Chronic Illness 85

Judgements: Illness, Cause, Cure 91

Cures come from Health 95

Appendix: A Cure Flowchart 101

The Meanings of Cure

Medically, cure is only defined in a testable fashion for a few infectious illnesses, cured by medically addressing the infectious agent.

Historically, the word cure has three main meanings: curing illness, a pastoral charge of a parish, and a process of curing substances like concrete and bacon. This book is about curing illness.

Cure, Cures, Curing, Cured

A cure is not a thing we can see or touch, not a substance, not a medicine. Even when we use the word cure and curative for a medicine that kills the cause of a disease, the cure comes from the action of taking the medicine as prescribed and the change caused by the medicine.

Cure (verb):

Cure: to bring about the end of an illness. A cure change might be a natural process, or a deliberate or even an accidental action. **cures**: performs the act of curing an illness. **curing**: removing or ending an illness. **cured**: The past tense of the verb cure.

Examples:

- The patient wants to cure their scurvy.
- The psychologist cures mental diseases.
- A healthy diet is credited with curing the scurvy.
- The dietary change cured the patient's scurvy.

Cure (noun):

cure: an change that brings about the end of an illness. **cures**: the plural of cure. **curing**: the act of ending an illness. **cured**: those patients who have cured their illnesses.

Examples:
- The cure for scurvy is a change in the patient's diet.
- There are many cures for scurvy, depending on the cause.
- The curing of a patient's scurvy took many days.
- The cured returned to their homes.

Cure (adjective):

cure: defines a process or action that cures. **cured**: the state of having been cured.

Example:
- The cure process was long and involved
- The cured patients danced and sang.

What is Cured?

Do we cure an illness, a disease, a sickness, a disorder, perhaps a medical condition, a disability, or something else? The following definitions are used in this book.

Cure is defined as *curing an illness*.

Illness: an illness is a negative medical condition *which can be cured*. If it cannot be cured, it is not a curable illness. When the word illness is used in this text, it refers to a curable condition.

> *A patient goes to a doctor with an illness,
> and goes home with a disease. -- unknown*

Disease: a disease is what a physician or medical professional diagnoses. Diseases are defined by medical professionals and include many curable and incurable conditions, disorders and disabilities.

Sickness: a sickness is a community or societal view of illness. A sickness might be an illness, or not; might be a disease, or not; might be curable, or not. For example, snoring be perceived as a sickness long before it is an illness, long before it should be diagnosed as a disease.

Disability: an incurable medical condition, disease, or disorder.

Ivan Illich, in the book **Medical Nemesis**, wrote: "Medicine has the authority to label one man's complaints (*illness*) a legitimate illness (*disease*)", to declare a second man sick (*diseased*) though he himself does not complain, and to refuse a third social recognition for his disability (*disease*).

Cure vs Treatment

Cures addresses cause and consequences of an illness. Signs and symptoms fade away as the illness is cured. Every illness is a single case; every cure is an anecdote.

Treatments for diseases and disabilities are often designed to suppress or mask the signs and symptoms of a disease — making no attempt to address cause, no attempt to cure the illness. Treatment effectiveness is measured statistically. We might study treatments forever, without learning to cure.

Most diseases cannot be cured. Due to the absence of a definition of cured, most disease cures cannot be tested much less proven when they occur. As a result, most disease cures are labelled *remission of signs and symptoms*, as if the disease is still present, but hiding.

This diagram illustrates some differences between elements of illness and cases of disease and the use of treatments vs cures.

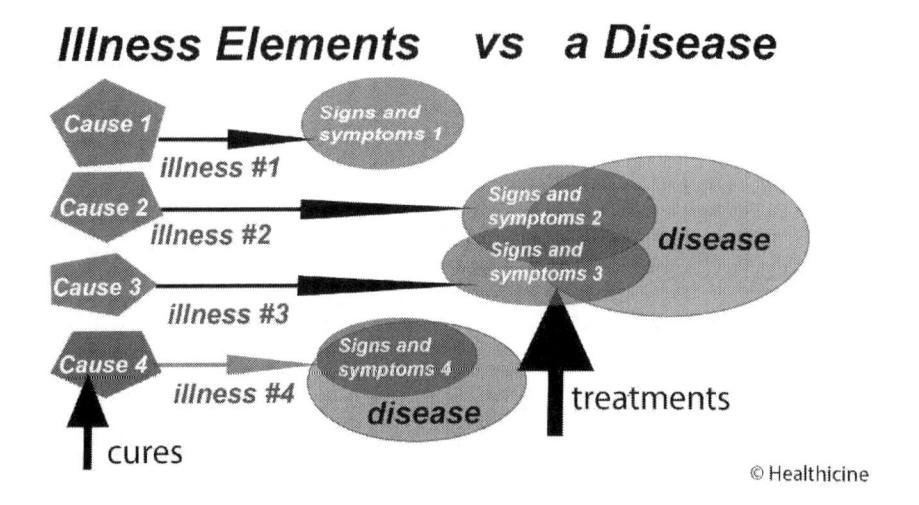

Illness Elements vs a Disease

Cause 1 → Signs and symptoms 1 — illness #1
Cause 2 → Signs and symptoms 2 — illness #2
Cause 3 → Signs and symptoms 3 — illness #3 — disease
Cause 4 → Signs and symptoms 4 — illness #4 — disease

cures ↑   treatments ↑

© Healthicine

A disease is a general concept that does not map perfectly to any illness or group of illnesses. A cure changes the cause. A treatment changes signs and symptoms.

Each illness element has a unique cause. Signs and symptoms of illnesses comprising a disease might be identical, similar, overlapping, or different.

Many diseases are diagnosed by signs and symptoms, without reference to cause. Many causes linked to diseases cannot be used to cure. Illnesses with overlapping signs and symptoms are often diagnosed as a single case of disease even when they have different causes, especially when the causal chains contain similar elements. In this diagram, one disease consists of two illness elements, illness 2 and illness 3. A disease can consist of a single illness, a group of illnesses, or might not be an illness. An illness might be a disease or not a diagnosable disease.

Illness

An illness is a hole in health, a judgement that an illness is present. We often deliberately diminish or deny illness as it progresses. Sometimes that's a healthy decision. Most illnesses are cured naturally, by natural healthy changes to body, mind, spirits, environments, or communities.

Illness is a Hole in a Healthiness

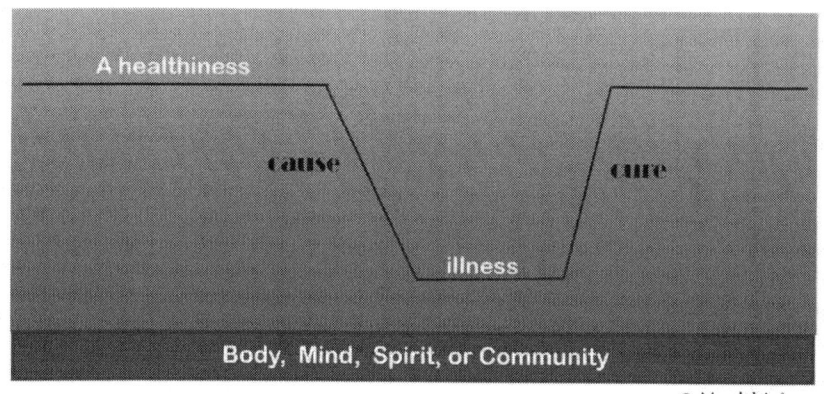

© Healthicine

Every illness has a cause, a change that causes the illness. An illness is an intersection of a cause and its negative consequences, having three parts:

- a cause,
- negative consequences, the signs and symptoms of illness,
- our understanding or belief that the cause is responsible for the consequences.

No illness is a *thing*. Illnesses do not come and go, cannot hide and resurface. Causes might wax and wane, come and go. Causes might be diminished and later strengthened or accumulate strength. They can create damage over time. Healthiness, defending against illness, also waxes and wanes naturally. Signs and symptoms, the negative effects of illness, rise and fall as cause and healthiness interact.

This is a book about curable illnesses. In this text an illness is *that which can be cured*. A condition that cannot be cured might be a disability, a handicap, or a natural attribute, to be accepted or dealt with, but not a curable illness.

An illness exists a consequence of negative judgement. A case of disease, sickness, disorder, or medical condition is also a negative judgement – by external individuals or communities. Disease, sickness, and medical conditions are also invisible concepts, not physical things. A case of disease only exists when diagnosed by a medical professional – although a diagnosis can be retroactive. An illness does not require a physician's judgement. A patient judges an illness to be present, or not.

Illness Element

An element of illness has a single cause. Two of the fundamental types of illness are based on a present cause. The third type of illness is an injury, where the cause is gone. When the cause is present, and the illness is cured by addressing the cause, often followed by healing. When cause is in the past, the cure is healing. A case of disease, a disorder or medical condition might consist of zero to many illness elements. When diseases are not cured, causes and illnesses can accumulate, growing in number and force.

Causal Illness: causal illnesses elements are caused by a life process or absence of process.

Examples:

- Scurvy can be caused by a severe dietary deficiency of Vitamin C.
- Shin splints can be caused by excessive running.

A causal illness is cured by addressing the process cause. Sometimes, two or more causes create similar, overlapping, or identical signs and symptoms. In these cases, there are two or more illness elements, which might be diagnosed as a single disease, but require multiple cures.

There are many ways to cure a causal illness, to change a process cause and produce a cure.

Attribute Illness: attribute illness elements are caused by the presence or absence of an attribute, which interferes with natural, healthy processes of life. The attribute has a cause, but that cause is in the past. Attribute illnesses are cured by transforming, or changing, the attribute cause.

Examples:

- Cataracts are blocked vision caused by clouding in the lens of the eye, cured by a surgical transformation.
- A dislocated shoulder is an absence of healthy, normal alignment, cured by a physical adjustment.

An attribute illness is cured by addressing or transforming the attribute cause. There are many ways to address any attribute cause to produce a cure. Transformations often cause damage – so attribute cures often require healing.

Injury: the cause of an injury is in the past. An injury illness element exists when a force or a stress results in an injury, which can be healed. Addressing the cause might prevent future injuries, but it cannot cure an injury. Injuries are cured by healing. The concept of an illness element is less important for injuries because injuries have a single cure.

Elementary Cures

Three cures are recognized by conventional medicine, although rarely documented as such. These are the cures explored in this book. No other cures exist.

Cure: to end an illness caused by an active process by addressing the causal process.

Heal: to end an injury, with a cause in the past, by the natural processes of health and healing.

Transform: to end an illness with a causal attribute in the present, by transforming the causal attribute.

Cure Proves Cause

Three Elements of Illness

causal illness, injury illness, attribute illness

© Healthicine

There is no simple distinction between the types of illness elements while the illness is present.

The type of an illness element is defined and proven by a cure. When a process change cures the illness, it was a causal illness element. When a transformation of an attribute cures, it was an attribute illness.

When healing cures an illness, it was an injury illness.

It is entirely possible for similar illnesses, diagnosed as the same disease, to be cured by a process in one case, by a transformation in another, and by healing in a third case. The cure defines and proves the cause.

The curability of an illness is proven by a cure. It is not possible to prove any illness incurable. Suggesting an illness is *incurable* is giving up.

Is Curing so Easy?

Is curing so easy that addressing any a single cause leads to a cure? So easy that every cause and every illness presents many opportunities to cure? At first glance, this seems inconceivable. There are two important keys to understanding.

From Illness Elements to Cures

This book is about elements of illness and elements of cure. Each illness element has a cause. Successfully addressing the cause is sufficient to cure that element of illness. Life is complex. Causes are many and varied. A cure element is a single action which addressing a single cause. Process cures, which address process causes, are processes must be maintained to maintain the cure. Attribute cures are single actions. Illnesses with multiple causes are multiple illness elements, requiring multiple cures.

Most Cures Are Natural

Most cures come from nature, from natural activities. If it were not so, humans would have died out centuries ago. Malnutrition occurs during a famine, causing many illnesses that are cured when food is plentiful. Other illnesses arrive when food is too plentiful, and fade with famine. The common cold, the flu, and measles, each viewed as incurable by conventional medicines, are cured by health. When we are healthier, we cure faster. When we are less healthy, cures take longer. Most illnesses are dangerous only when severe unhealthiness is present. Most injuries are minor. Healing cures without conscious intention.

Diseases

A disease is a generalized class of illness, identified and recognized by a medical profession, often without reference to cause. Simple illnesses are often cured by health. Most diseases are complex or compound illnesses, requiring multiple cures.

We notice diseases because they persist. When, illnesses are not cured, they can accumulate causes, becoming more difficult to cure. We ignore naturally cured illnesses. Medical professionals focus attention on diseases not easily cured by health, those persisting long enough to require a doctor's attention.

Secondary Illness

An illness caused by illness is a secondary illness. If the prior illness is still present, two illnesses exist, although they might be diagnosed as a single disease – two cures are required, one for each illness.

Complex Illness

A complex illness exists when a present illness causes other illnesses, or when a single cause produces multiple illness elements.

Examples:

- Scurvy can cause injuries to bones, teeth and gums
- A wound injury might cause or allow an infection to grow
- An attribute illness, like cataracts, might cause chronic falls and injuries

A complex illness requires multiple cures, one for each illness element. When scurvy is caught before it causes injuries, it can be cured easily, so it is seldom diagnosed as scurvy – we call it Vitamin C deficiency.

Sometimes, an illness with a present cause causes illness or injury. In these cases, a cure of the secondary illness might not last. Two or more cures are required.

Example:
- A damaged tendon in the back might cause an imbalance in the shoulders, creating tension in the upper arm and forearm, producing an illness – signs and symptoms of pain or numbness in the fingers. Curing a chain of illness might require a cure at each link of the chain, some of which might be not perceived as an illness by the patient.

Compound Illness

A compound illness is an illness with multiple present causes and similar or overlapping signs and symptoms, requiring two or more actions cure.

There is an important distinction to be made between a complex and a compound illness. A compound illness is like a disease with multiple causes. Sometimes, even before a disease is diagnosed, causes accumulate, increasing the number and severity of illnesses.

How do we know if an illness is simple or compound? When more than one cause must be addressed to cure it is a compound illness.

Example:
- A patient might suffer from malnutrition, causing scurvy because they are poor and also addicted to drugs or alcohol. Addressing the poverty cause alone will not address the addiction, the scurvy illness will persist. Addressing the addiction cause alone will not address the poverty, the malnutrition illness will persist. This patient has (at least)

two illness elements because two cures are required to address the poverty and addiction.

The concept of a compound illness is critical to curing. Conventional medicine views many diseases as caused by multiple factors but makes few attempts to cure. Today, there is no medical concept of a compound disease, requiring two or more cures.

Successfully addressing a single cause cures an illness element. However, when an illness is compound, addressing a cause only produces a partial cure, which is seldom recognized as a cure. Patients and doctors might give up, allowing the cause to return or recur.

Chronic Illness

A chronic illness has a chronic cause. Chronic is an attribute of the cause. An illness element is chronic when the cause persists over time. We can create many illnesses by creating the cause. We can create chronic illnesses by creating an illness with a chronic cause. Chronic illnesses often emerge from unhealthy diets, routines, or habits of body, mind, spirits, or communities.

A chronic causal illness is caused by a chronic unhealthy process. Many causes do not cause illness until they are chronic. Obesity is caused, not by overeating, but by chronic overeating. A chronic causal illness can only be cured by addressing the chronic nature of the cause.

Attribute illnesses are usually chronic because attribute causes are naturally chronic, existing in time. A hernia, or a cataract, persists. They cannot be healed. But they can be cured. Some attribute illnesses, notably those with causes in community or environment, are chronic until the attribute changes. Someone with SAD (Seasonal Affective Disorder) will find their illness is cured when they move to the tropics where the climate has different attributes.

Repetitive stress injuries are chronic injuries resulting from chronic often minor stressful actions.

When healthiness is low, an illness which can only be cured by improving healthiness might occur. Chronic unhealthiness can cause chronic causal illnesses, chronic attribute illnesses, or chronic injury illnesses which are each cured by improving healthiness.

Conventional medicine views chronic illnesses as incurable, a combination of medical chauvinism and a failure to understand the chronic nature of many causes of illness.

Iatrogenic Illnesses

An iatrogenic illness is one caused by a diagnostic process, a treatment, or a cure. Most medical treatments make no attempt to cure. In some cases, adverse medical consequences, often called *side effects,* are minor and easily tolerated. In other cases, they become illnesses. Iatrogenic damage is often studied but rarely called a disease.

Most medicines are toxic by design. Properly prescribed, they seldom cause iatrogenic illnesses. Many iatrogenic illnesses are due to medical errors.

Degenerative Illnesses

Curable degenerative illnesses are chronic conditions that slowly create more damage until they cured. The damage might include injuries, negative attributes, even disabilities. Degenerative diseases are often curable chronic illnesses that are allowed to persist, causing disabilities which cannot be cured.

Examples:

- Type 1 Diabetes is viewed as a degenerative disease, due to a disability, a negative attribute that cannot be changed – the absence of islet cells.
- Type 2 Diabetes, on the other hand, is viewed as a degenerative disease caused by the patient's life choices. As a result, Type 1 Diabetes is viewed as an incurable degenerative disease, not a curable illness. Type 2 Diabetes is a potentially curable degenerative illness. However, today's medical practice does not have any technique to recognize a cure of any type of diabetes when it occurs.

It is important to emphasize *viewed as*. Type 1 Diabetes and Type 2 Diabetes are complex and varied. It might be possible for one patient to have an incurable Type 1 Diabetes, a disability, while another patient has a curable Type 1 Diabetes, a curable illness. We cannot know for certain until we succeed in curing. It is also possible for one patient to have an incurable Type 2 Diabetes illness, while another has a curable Type 2 Diabetes illness.

Repeating Illness

An illness repeats when the cause is repeating. The distinction between a chronic illness and a repeating illness is a judgement. A chronic illness waxes and wanes as the cause grows and shrinks, and as healing brings recovery. A repeating illness is cured when the cause is addressed. A new illness occurs when the cause returns. The concept of a repeating disease, as opposed to chronic, does not exist in conventional medicine, because cured is seldom recognized. A repeating illness requires repeating cures.

Incurable Illness?

A medical condition judged to be incurable might be a disease, a disability, a handicap, or a natural feature. Often a decision, diagnosis, or medical practice judges a condition to be incurable. If it is subsequently cured or judged to be curable, it has been transformed by the presence of a cure, into a curable illness. However, conventional medicine generally ignores these situations by simply ignoring cures.

A medical condition judged to be incurable might be a disease, but not a curable illness. It has become a condition which must be accepted. A patient whose leg is blown off by an explosion has a disability, not a curable illness. Of course, until their injury is healed, they also have an injury illness. If we someday learn to regrow the leg, it might be converted to a curable illness.

An illness, when judged to be incurable, becomes a reality that must be accepted, perhaps treated. Cataracts were judged a disability until we learned to cure them with surgery. Specific cases might still be judged as an incurable disability.

Body, Mind, Spirit, and Community Illnesses

The cause of an illness might be in the body of the patient or the patient's actions, in the mind of the patient, in their knowledge and beliefs, in their spirits, their intentions, motivations, and goals. The cause might come from a patient's community or their environments. Every patient lives in multiple communities. Each has many layers of internal and external environments.

Consequences of an illness include positive and negative effects on body, mind, spirit, and community. We judge an illness to be negative, but not every consequence of every illness is negative.

The diagram on the next page shows the hierarchy of healthicine as potential sources of causes of illness. An illness might occur in any area or in any boundary between different areas in the diagram.

Consequences of an illness can have negative effects on many areas — even far away from the cause in location and in time.

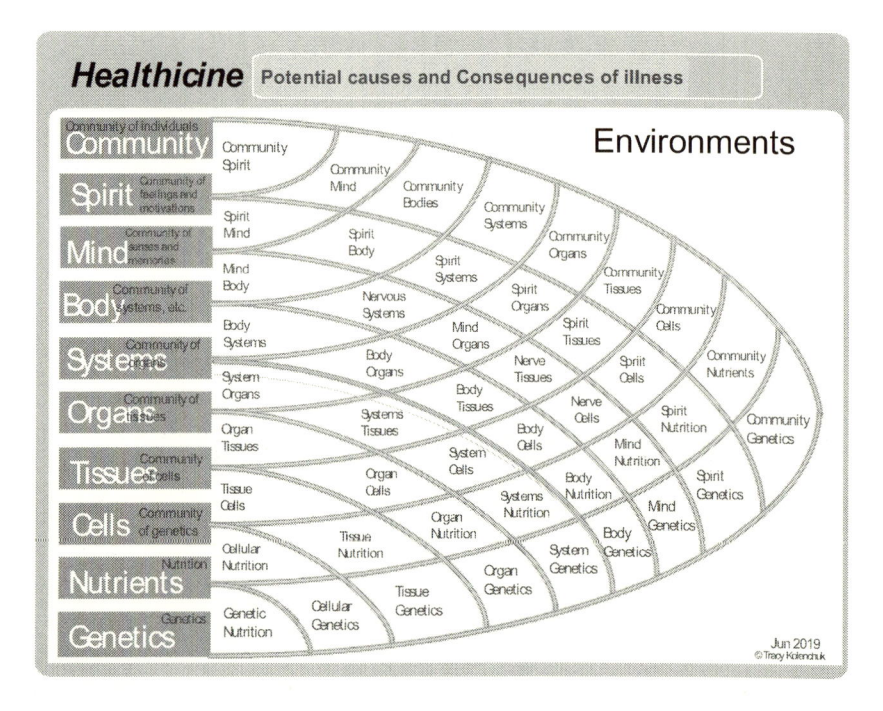

Healthicine — Potential causes and Consequences of illness

Each layer in the hierarchy of healthicine consists of individual elements, which emerge through communities of cooperation from the layers below. An illness might be caused by failures in natural processes of competition and cooperation, by flaws in elements, or by injuries.

Causes of Illness

There are three elementary causes of illness. Each leads to a different type of illness, requiring a different type of cure. When a causal or an attribute illness element exists, the cause is present such that successfully addressing the cause, cures.

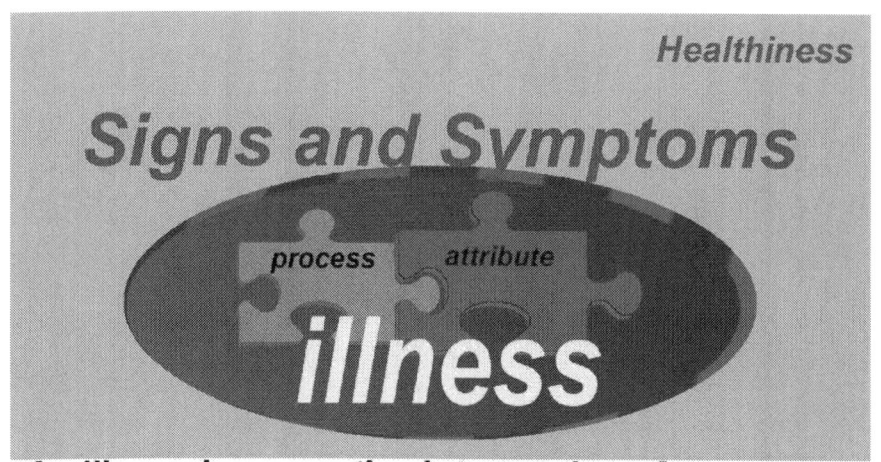

An illness is a negative intersection of a process and an attribute, creating a hole in healthiness.
© Healthicine

An illness with a present cause exists when the ongoing consequences of a life process and an attribute (which might also be a process) is negative, resulting in signs and symptoms of illness. Either the process or the attribute might be seen as the cause.

We can view the description of a present illness as a sentence:

The *process* (subject) interacts with an *attribute* (object) resulting in *negative consequences* (the illness). Sometimes we might phrase it differently, such that "The *attribute* interferes with a *process*, resulting in *negative consequences* (the illness)."

We will find cures in the process or the attribute cause, but not in the consequences.

Process Cause

Life is a process with many layers of process in body, mind, spirits, and communities. When processes fail, the result might be illness or death. Processes rarely fail catastrophically. Life processes wax and wane, by design. All of our life processes must maintain many active balances and harmonies to maintain healthiness. When a process becomes too active, inactive, or inharmonious, a causal illness can result.

Attribute Cause

Life's processes interact with our physical, mental, spirit, and community attributes. We walk by manipulating the balances of our body by falling and recovering. This common movement depends on many physical attributes. When our balancing (a process), or our leg muscles (an attribute), are deficient or dysfunctional, we might fall.

Boundaries are attributes, essential to life. When boundaries are excessive or deficient, the unhealthy attribute can block natural healthy life processes.

Stress or Force Causes

Healthy interaction of life processes and attributes creates stress. Life uses force and stress to advantage. However, when stresses are excessive, sometimes when they are deficient, injuries can occur. Stresses of body, mind, spirit, community, or environment might cause injuries. Excessive force can come from a negative process or an interaction with a negative attribute.

Distinguishing Between Cause Types

Three Fundamental Causes of Illness

process (function)
force (stress)
attribute (form)

© Healthicine

There are no clear distinctions between process, attribute, and force causes. We make distinctions to facilitate cures. When an illness is cured by a process, it was a causal illness. When cured by healing, it was an injury; a force caused illness. When cured by a transformation, it was an attribute illness.

Until the illness is cured, we cannot be certain of the cause. Once an illness is cured, we might be wrong, but a cure is a cure.

Cure Cause

A cure is an action that cures an illness. The cure cause is the one which, when addressed, results in a cure. Causal illness elements are cured by a change that addresses a process cure cause on an ongoing basis. Attribute illness elements are cured by a change that transforms an attribute cure cause. Injury illnesses are cured by the processes of healing. Each curable illness has many potential cure causes, many alternative ways to be cured.

Duality of Cause

Every process and every attribute cause has two sides. Every cause has a dual nature, consisting of the force of the cause vs. healthiness - the resistance, the strength and defences of the patient. Some medical theories refer to the disease and the terrain. Naturopathy and homeopathy often refer to the terrain which, although poorly defined, often means the healthiness of the patient, with regards to the illness. We might view these two sides as inside and outside; however, life consists of many layers, from genetics to cells, tissues, organs, organ systems, body, mind, spirit, and community. Each layer can be an internal or external environment for other layers.

When a cause is too strong, it overwhelms the patient causing an illness. When the patient is weak or injured, a lesser cause is dangerous. Both sides of this duality change over time, waxing and waning. As a result, it can be difficult to know which side contains a cure cause. A cure proves the cause. If the illness was cured by addressing a cause, that was the cause. If the illness is cured by improving the health of the patient, a lack of healthiness was the cause. We might argue otherwise, but a cure is a proof.

The duality of cause is not limited to physicality. The internal side, the healthiness side of every cause has a physical duality, a mind duality, a spirit duality, and a community duality. When we are physically healthier, a cause might not result in illness. When we are mentally healthier, a cause might not produce an illness. When our spirits are healthier, a cause might not harm us. When we have the support of a healthier community, illnesses are less common, more easily cured.

Other Concepts of Cause

There are many ways to study cause and effect, although few are relevant to curing. Philosophical analysis of cause and effect often constrains causes to events in the past. Active illnesses have causes in the present. Present causes can be fractal. A present cause often has a present *cause of a cause*, which has a present *cause of a cause of a cause*.

Sufficient and Necessary Causes

Causes of disease are often studied by epidemiologists, with aims of prevention. Epidemiologists use the sufficient-component cause model to prevent, but not to cure diseases. Cure is not defined in epidemiology. Curing any non-injury illness requires addressing a present cause, not a statistical cause.

Proximate and Ultimate Causes

A proximate cause is one closest to an event, a higher-level ultimate cause or distal cause is one generally judged to be the cause of an event. However, causal and attribute illnesses are a consequence of life's processes, not single events. Proximate and distal classifications although important for prevention of injuries are less useful to cure.

The concepts of proximal and ultimate causes can be adapted to curing causal illnesses. A proximal cause being one so close to the signs and symptoms that addressing it does not cure. An ultimate cause, or distal cause, being a cure cause.

For example, a causal illness:

- Scurvy is caused by a bodily deficiency of Vitamin C. This is a proximal cause, closest to the disease. Vitamin C supplements will not cure. Signs and symptoms will go into remission until the medicine is stopped, and then return. The illness was never cured.
- A distal, ultimate, or cure cause is the diet of the patient. When the patient's diet is successfully changed, the scurvy is cured.

The concepts of proximal and ultimate causes are less useful to cure attribute illnesses. The cause of the attribute is in the past. The attribute or its absence is the cure cause, which must be transformed to cure.

Trigger Causes

The concept of a trigger cause is frequently encountered in medicine, although poorly, often inconsistently defined. A trigger suggests a small event that releases a lot of damage. However, in conventional medicine, the word trigger has many meanings and is often confused with cause. An infection might be said to be triggered by an injury, even a small scratch. Triggers are often described as *"the straw that broke the camel's back."* But a trigger is rarely a cure cause.

A trigger is a simple stress or change that pushes an unhealthiness past an illness boundary. Triggering is often the final breakdown of a defence that has been maintained for some time. An unhealthiness causes minor damage. Invisible danger creeps higher and higher. At some point, a threshold is reached. Suddenly a small change triggers a catastrophe.

A triggered illness has two parts: an *illness in waiting* sometimes *in remission* and an event, possibly a minor stress or illness, that releases the pressure. There are two ways to cure a trigger illness. When we view the presence of a trigger as an attribute cause, we avoid the trigger. Many people learn to avoid certain triggers. However, avoiding a trigger does not address the underlying issue. There is often a danger another trigger will emerge, or an illness will occur without a clear trigger.

The best cure for a triggered illness is to address the cause of the underlying unhealthiness – which might not be seen as an illness. This cure might be invisible, only becoming apparent over time, when the trigger fails to cause another instance of illness. Proving a hidden illness cured requires confidence that a cure cause has been addressed.

Causal Chains

Every cause of an illness element is part of a chain of causes, part of the processes of life. Every cause has a cause, and every consequence of a cause might be a cause of illness. A causal illness has a present and active causal chain. For injury illnesses, the cause is gone. Studying injury causal chains is useful for prevention. For attribute illnesses, the cause of the attribute might be present, or in the past. When the cause is present, changing the attribute might only provide a temporary cure.

Not all causes are negative. There are causes of healthiness, causes of cures, and causes of joy. Life entities survive, grow, reproduce and evolve by manipulating cause and effect.

Humans think deeply about cause and effect. When we examine any cause of illness, we find a cause of the cause and a cause of the cause of the cause. As we dig deeper, we can find consequences of each cause, which might be important in our search for a cure. Any curable illness has many possibilities to be cured.

There are no root causes. There is a famous story of a science professor giving a lecture on the solar system. At the end of the lecture, an elderly person stood up and exclaimed *"This is all garbage. The world sits on the back of a turtle."* The professor asked, quietly, *"What does the turtle stand on, then?"*. *"Another turtle, of course."* Exclaimed the elder. *"It's turtles all the way down."*

Causal chains are fractal. Every cause has a cause. Every consequence becomes a cause. There are no root causes. It's causes all the way down. Life uses cause and effect to live. We find the useful cause by curing. The important cause is the one that cures, a cure cause.

Process Causal Chains

In a process causal chain, each causal link is necessary to create the illness element. When a single link is addressed, the chain is broken. The illness is cured. However, addressing a process cause, curing a causal illness, requires ongoing maintenance or termination of the process.

Attribute Causal Chains

An attribute is a thing, which might be a faulty process. Blindness is an attribute that might lead to accidents and illness. An attribute has a cause in the past, which has a cause in the past, which has a cause in the past. In some cases, when an attribute causing an illness is transformed, it might later be re-created. In these cases, we need to address the visible attribute and search for the cause that creates the attribute. This might occur when bodily parts are out of alignment, such that they create a chain of misalignments until one is perceived as an illness. It can also occur due to mental, spirit, or community processes or attributes. Working through a chain of causes must often be completed in a proper sequence.

Process or Attribute Cause?

Causal chains might link from processes to attributes, and from attributes to processes, again and again. Successfully addressing any link in a causal chain can produce a cure. We might cure an illness with a process cure or with an attribute cure – depending on the causal link we address. For example:

- A patient is suffering scurvy because they are poor and cannot afford healthy food. The illness might be cured by an attribute, by a job, or it might be cured by an ongoing process, by providing them with an income such that they can afford healthy food. The successful cure identifies the cause.

Once an illness is cured, we might speculate that another cure might also have provided a cure. But the illness has been cured. Processes cure changes must be maintained, attribute cure changes are permanent.

An illness with Two Causes?

A complex or compound illness can have multiple causes. But, by definition: *an illness element* has a single cause. Illness elements are cured one at a time.

Sometimes, the causal chain splits in two. A single cause might be seen as having two prior causes necessary to produce the cause. We use simple rules to understand these situations and find cures.

- An illness element has a single causal chain. Successfully addressing any link in the causal chain produces a cure.
- If multiple causes must be addressed to cure, the patient has multiple illnesses. A single cure action cures a single element, producing an elementary cure, which might be invisible if signs and symptoms of illness are still present.
- Every individual action necessary to cure an illness indicates the presence of an elementary illness.

What if an illness element has exactly two causes, each necessary to cause the illness? This is not possible. It is an error in the definition of an element of illness. Disease is defined by signs and symptoms, which often leads to a failure to cure. Curable illness is defined by cause, not by signs or symptoms. An illness element has a single cause. Causes are hypothetical at diagnosis, proven at cure.

When a causal chain splits in two, cures multiply in number and divide in results.

Example:

- A person might suffer depression with two causes – physical and emotional abuse from a roommate and also a faulty diet. Addressing the abuse cause, but not addressing the unhealthy diet provides only a partial cure. Addressing the unhealthy diet, but not the abuse, also provides only a partial cure. In both cases, the cure might be visible as an improvement, or invisible.
- If the person moves to a new city, gets a new job and a new circle of friends, both the abuse and the unhealthy diet might be addressed. A single cure action converted the compound illness, having two independent causes, into an illness element, with a single cause and a single cure.

The cause of an illness element is proven by the cure.

Causal Illness:

When a person has a causal illness element with two or more potential process causes, each of which is *necessary* to maintain the illness, addressing any of the causes will result in a cure.

When a patient has an illness with two causes, both of which must be addressed to cure the illness, the patient has two illness elements, because two cures actions are required.

Attribute Illness:

Attribute illness causes are not active. The illness arises from the patient's life interactions with the attribute. When a patient has two negative attributes appearing to cause an illness, and both attributes are necessary to maintain the illness, addressing either will cure.

A cure element cures a single illness element, by addressing a single causal attribute. When two cures were required, there were two illnesses elements to be cured. A single active illness might have both attribute and process causes in the causal chain, but there can only be a single cure. Cure proves cause.

Injury Illness:

When a patient has an injury illness, the cause is gone, no longer relevant to curing. A patient might have a broken arm because of a fall, which might have been broken further when they were clumsily loaded into the ambulance. The number of causes is irrelevant to cure. Healing of injuries proceeds without regard for cause. Sometimes we judge an injury to be two illnesses, or more if multiple healing processes are necessary.

Locating A Cause

Causal chains are not restricted to the physical layers of life. Every cause is an effect of a prior cause. A cause in body, mind, spirit, community or environment might produce an effect, which becomes the next cause in the chain, in body, mind, spirit, or community.

Example:

- A patient suffering from a deficiency of Vitamin C might have a cause in their diet – body – which has a cause in their job – their community. A parent or family member might blame the cause on their mind or spirit, on their inability to believe or to be motivated to change jobs. There is always room to speculate about cause before the cure. Only a cure can prove a cause.

Many medical practitioners refer to body, mind, and spirit – often missing community and environment layers. We need also be aware that a human body consists of many layers, from genetics to cells, to tissues, to organs and organ systems. Entities in each layer in the hierarchy are communities, and also part of the environment for other layers.

Perhaps, as we study healthicine and cures, we will learn to distinguish important layers in mind, spirit, and community.

A cause can occur at any level, or in any community, the transitions between levels, and at any intersection entities in different levels. Consequences can affect the entire hierarchy.

Layer	Affects
Environment	an environment for all lower layers
Community	a community of individuals of body, mind, and spirit, and an environment for individuals.
Body: Individual consisting of body, mind, and spirits.	a community of body components and an environment for all body parts.
Organ System	a community of organs and tissues and also an environment for organs and tissues.
Organ	a community of tissues and cells and an environment for tissues and cells.
Tissue	a community of different cell types and an environment for cells.
Cell	a community of chemical and genetic components and processes.
Nutrients	Nutrients are required for life, health, and reproduction of cells.

Deficiencies or Excesses?

Are all diseases a result of deficiency or excess? There are important differences between illnesses caused by deficiencies and those caused by excesses. Understanding these differences is essential to cure and essential to understanding when a cure has been accomplished.

Each of the three basic types of cause: processes, attributes, and stresses, might be deficient or excessive. Any life process might become deficient or excessive. Dietary intake might be deficient or excessive, leading to illness or injury. Exercise or rest of body, mind, spirit, or community might be deficient or excessive, leading to illness or injury of body, mind, spirit or community of the patient. Attributes that are excessive, deficient, or missing, from body, to mind, to spirits, to communities, can lead to many different illnesses.

We naturally suffer many minor injuries as a result of life and living. Healing processes are constantly active. Deficiencies or excesses of healing can also lead to illness and injury. Deficiencies or excesses of healthy exercise or stress can also lead to deficiencies of health and healing.

> *Life don't clickety clack down a straight-line track*
> *It comes together and it comes apart.*
> *--- Ferron*

Deficiency Illnesses

Deficiencies causes of illness have an important feature related to curing. Most deficiencies are always in-waiting. Conventional medicine ignores the processes causing deficiency often addressing the deficiency directly – resulting in a false cure, a remission of signs and symptoms. Currently, cured is not medically defined for any deficiency disease.

Process Cause Example:

- A minor deficiency of Vitamin C causes "Vitamin C deficiency" which is rarely diagnosed.
- A severe deficiency of Vitamin C causes the disease scurvy. Many references suggest that scurvy is best treated by supplementation with Vitamin C. This type of error is often made with deficiency causes. Supplemental Vitamin C addresses signs and symptoms, facilitates and promotes healing. However, as soon as the medicine is stopped, the signs and symptoms reappear. No cure cause was addressed.
- In many cases, for example, infantile scurvy, the disease is cured by natural changes in diet as the child grows – the supplementation appears to produce a cure. Medical chauvinism takes credit. The true cause is easily ignored after a natural cure.

Even in illnesses caused by a non-physical deficiency, conventional medicine easily confuses remission and cure.

Attribute Cause Example:

- A deficiency of sunlight in winter can cause Seasonal Affective Disorder (SAD). When spring comes, it appears the illness has gone into remission and will return the next winter. No. It has been cured. Deficiency illnesses do not *"go into remission."* They exist when the deficiency is present and are cured when the deficiency is addressed. We might say they had the potential for SAD after the winter has passed. Perhaps they always had this potential, without any illness. Someone with the potential for SAD will not get the illness if they move to a tropical climate where the deficiency cause does not exist. Anyone might have the potential for SAD, whether they have had the illness in the past or not.

Some deficiencies are so dangerous we don't call them illnesses. If someone stops breathing, they don't get an illness, they die. Others are tolerated for long periods or countered by other health factors. Many people can go for years on very little sleep, while others require significantly more sleep to avoid illness.

Health is flexible and adaptable. It's a necessity of life. Many deficiencies can be met in different ways. A jungle resident might get plenty of Vitamin C from the fruits and vegetables of the jungle. An arctic resident gets necessary amounts from raw meat.

A deficiency illness is cured when the cause of the deficiency is addressed, when healing of injuries has completed, and when no more medicines are required. If the cause occurs again, the result is a new case of illness, not remission and reemergence. An illness is a concept, not something that can go away and return.

Stress Illnesses

We seldom call an illness caused by excess an "*illness of excess*" we use the word *stress*. We often refer to illnesses caused by excessive community involvement or responsibility as caused by stress. Every illness is a result of stress. We can view any stress illness as a result of deficiency or excess of a process or attribute. Even a deficiency is a stress. However, a deficiency stress is due to an absence, not an excess.

Stress and risk are essential to life. Without stress, there is no life, no movement, no growth, no health. The more stress we can use to our advantage, the more strength, ability, and potential we have in life.

How much stress is required to cause an illness? The amount that produces an illness. An excess of stress exists when stress overwhelms the strength and health of the individual. Every individual has different levels of strength and health, which are constantly changing. Healthiness and illness are about the individual, or about the individual community in cases of a community illness.

Stress illnesses often provide two paths to cure. It is possible to cure the illness by addressing or reducing the stress. In these cases, if the stress reoccurs, a new case of illness will occur. It is also possible, in many cases, to cure a stress caused illness by strengthening the patient, such that the stress does not cause illness. If the patient weakens at a later date, they will develop a new case of illness. The original illness was cured when the cause was addressed. The new illness will require a new cure, which might be the same cure action, repeated.

A stress illness is cured when the cause is successfully addressed when healing has completed when no more medicines are needed for signs and symptoms.

Sometimes, a deficiency of stress leads to illness. Healthy exercise is a stress. When we don't get enough, our bodies deteriorate, causing an illness.

Bedsores can be a deficiency illness. Care workers might cure bedsores by regularly moving a patient. We might wordsmith it as a stress illness *"caused by the stress of being confined to a bed."* Other patients might cure bedsores *"caused by a deficiency of exercise"* with increased exercise.

All illnesses are caused by stress!

All illnesses are caused by deficiencies.

Deficiencies are stressful. A deficiency is a stress!

A stress is just a deficiency of healthiness.

Photo: Tracy O'Camera

Consequences of Illness

Our health naturally reacts to causes of illness, often successfully countering them without any illness. However, this can sometimes place other life systems in stress, pushing them out of balance. Signs and symptoms of an illness might appear far from the cause. Addressing signs and symptoms often fails, even as it appears to be working.

Signs and Symptoms

It is important to understand that there are signs and symptoms of healthiness, as well as signs and symptoms of illness. *"I feel great!"* is a sign, a symptom. Spring fever is a sign of vitality, of health.

Signs and symptoms of illnesses are negative consequences of the illness, which provide valuable information about the illness. Masking signs and symptoms is a deliberate action to minimize or hide some aspects of the illness. It can be helpful for short-term illnesses, harmful in the long-term, seldom moving an illness towards cured.

Only an illness can be cured. Signs and symptoms are not cured. Conventional medicine makes weak distinctions between signs and symptoms and disease, due to inattention to cause. We must distinguish between causes, illness, signs and symptoms, and consequences to cure.

Example:

- Depression can be a sign or a symptom. It can also be a disease diagnosed without cause. Without a cause, it cannot be cured.

Negative signs and symptoms, which are not addressed by a cure, might indicate another element of illness needing to be cured, or a non-illness, a disability, handicap, or natural feature which cannot be cured. We might experience or observe many signs and symptoms we cannot connect to a cause. It can be difficult to determine if specific signs and symptoms indicate illness or natural healthiness. We might cough because of a cold, an illness, or cough because water went down the windpipe – a healthy cough. Doctors typically measure several signs and symptoms (but rarely causes) to diagnose a disease.

We are often uncertain which signs and symptoms are linked to an individual cause. We prove a link by curing an illness. Even then, we're never perfectly certain. When the illness is cured, does certainty matter?

Cures and treatments have positive and negative effects on a patient's health, often called adverse consequences or side effects. Every action to improve healthiness consists of give and take. Negative effects of a cure are, like every illness, judgements. A cure for our cold or influenza might mean we can no longer pamper ourselves in bed reading a book. People with chronic illnesses are often attached to the chronic nature of their illness or its cause. They unconsciously, sometimes consciously, do not want to be cured. Love your Disease, It's Keeping you Healthy by Dr. John Harrison explores this extensively.

Causal cures can decrease enjoyment. Healing cures often have side effects while the cure process is active – congestion, leakage, itchiness, or pain. Cures by transformation have many effects because they entail significant changes to body, mind, spirits, or communities, insignificant changes being less likely to cure.

Leakage and Congestion

Leakage and congestion are common consequences of injury and illness, which can also cause further injuries and illnesses.

Congestion occurs when a natural flow is blocked, or when a natural or unhealthy flow cannot be released or cleared. It can occur when a flow is excessive, or when the walls constraining a flow are inflexible. Internal leakages can also cause congestion. Congestion is not limited to physical congestion. Our minds become congested when our spirits are depressed, blocking healthy actions. Our spirits can become congested when we have too much on our mind, too many intentions, goals, or objectives to remember when we lose focus.

Congestion or leakage sometimes arrives rapidly. Other times they grow slowly, imperceptibly, progressing as we grow older, accumulating and building force. They might remain hidden for long periods, being cleared by natural, healthy processes, until an action blocks a healthy flow, or until a process flows faster than it can be cleared.

The cause might be internal or external. Until cause is addressed, the illness will persist. The problem will return. Many simple illnesses cause temporary blockages or leakages, leading to temporary congestion, which is cleared naturally by healthy activities and healing.

Today's medical practice, in general, is to treat signs and symptoms. Congestion is often viewed as a symptom and treated with a decongestant, a symptomicine. Sometimes an illness is short-term – like the common cold –a symptomicine is appropriate and effective. At other times, like high blood pressure, treating congestion, while ignoring the cause, allows illness to persist, grow, allowing causes to accumulate and multiply. Like all signs and symptoms, congestion speaks to us, providing valuable information about the underlying illness. When we suppress symptoms, we might fail to understand and fail to cure. No medical professional would advise a patient to *"learn to live with their congestion"* while many advise a patient to *"learn to live with their high blood pressure"* by taking daily medicines. High blood pressure is a symptom of illness, a congestion, due to unhealthiness in the blood vessels. It might be cured with health, but not with medicines.

Congestion or leakage might be a result of a disability, a handicap, or a natural attribute which cannot be cured. We might need to continually clear congestion or leakage from a disability because we cannot cure it.

Congestion might be a chronic symptom of a disability, persisting and recurring as long as the patient lives.

Spring Fever is not a disease: the restlessness of spring is a sign of change, and a symptom of healthiness.

Photo: Tracy O'Camera

Illness over Time

The consequences of a cause of illness, even of curing an illness might be immediate or they might not occur until some time after the cause or cure.

Infectious diseases that kill rapidly are rare – they work themselves out of susceptible victims. Infectious diseases that we can adapt to survive and evolve forward with us. The most effective infectious diseases are relatively innocuous – like the common cold.

Non-infectious diseases sometimes develop new negative consequences after years of minor signs and symptoms.

As we study cures, we must learn to understand these differences.

Cure

To resolve an illness by addressing a cause. Cause is defined by cure.

An illness element has a single cause. Illnesses are cured one element at a time. Complex and compound illnesses require multiple cures, one for each illness element, one for each cause.

The three types of illness elements have three types of causes and three corresponding types of cures: curing, healing and transforming.

Curing:

Changes to ongoing processes cures causal illness elements. An illness element cured by an ongoing process to address a cause was causal illness element. Improving healthiness improves causal cures.

Healing:

Injury illnesses are cured by health and healing. There are no other cures for injury illnesses. Healthy nutrition, rest, exercise, protection, cleansing, and many other actions can, aid but cannot cause curing. Healing progresses depending on the healthiness of the patient, irrespective of cause, except when the illness is a result of problems in the processes of healing. Improving healthiness improves healing cures.

Transforming:

Attribute illness elements are cured by transformations that change the causal attribute, removing a negative attribute, adding a missing attribute, or by strengthening or weakening an attribute. An illness element cured by a transformation was an attribute illness element. Improving healthiness improves transformational cures.

Curing with Health

Often, an illness is cured by an improvement in healthiness. In these cases, we are less certain if it was a causal, an injury, or an attribute illness. But a cure is a cure.

The Three Cures

Just as there are no clear distinctions between different causes and types of illness, there are no clear lines between the different elements of curing. We make decisions about a cure action when we aim to cure. If the decision, the cure action, is correct, the illness element will be cured. If not, we can use the knowledge provided by the failure to plan new cure attempt.

Three Elementary Cures of Illness

curing   healing

transforming

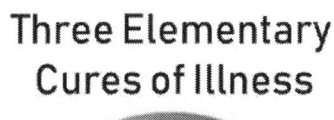

© Healthicine

Success proves a cure. When a cure succeeds, we know what illness type was present. When we fail, we have less certainty.

Cured

There are three basic conditions necessary for a cure. An illness is cured:

1. When the cause has been successfully addressed.
2. When the signs and symptoms of the illness have faded away.
3. When no more medicines are necessary.

Conventional medicine has only a single test for cured. An infection is cured when the parasite is demonstrated to have been disabled or removed. Which perfectly matches the first cure statement *"an illness is cured when the cause has been successfully addressed."*

There is no scientific medical definition of cured for any non-infectious disease. Alzheimer's, arthritis, bloat, cancer, depression, diabetes, epilepsy, fibromyalgia, gout, hypertension, inflammatory bowel disease (IBD), lupus, multiple sclerosis (MS), obesity, Parkinson's, even scurvy, and many more are technically incurable due to the absence of a definition of cured.

Chronic diseases are generally considered incurable in conventional medicine, a simple but common error. Chronic illnesses are caused by a chronic attribute, the chronic nature of a process, attribute, or stress. Few medical treatments address the chronic nature of a cause. The main exception being surgery, in which cases the disease is seldom viewed as a true chronic disease.

The Diagnostic and Statistical Manual of Mental Disorders (DSM-5) defines mental diseases. All mental diseases can currently be considered incurable due to the absence of a definition of cured. The reason is a definitional Catch-22. If a mental disorder is cured, in conventional medicine, it was cured by something physical. Therefore, it was not a mental illness. Mental disorders can only exist as long as they are incurable. Sometimes a mental illness is cured by surgery, by a physical transformation of the brain. Surgery is often considered a cure, but there is no medical test for, no scientific proof of cured or not, after a surgery.

Sometimes a psychologist, a priest, or a grandmother cures an illness of mind or spirit through conversation transforming mind or spirit to produce a cure. These cures are not recognized by conventional medicine, because a medical treatment does not produce them.

The common cold, influenza, measles, and many more diseases are commonly cured by health – not recognized as medical cures. There is no proof of cured for any disease cured by healthiness. As we study cures, we will learn that the best cure for any illness is to improve the health of the patient. Cures come from health, not medicines.

At present, few cures are recognized by conventional medicine – only those seen as brought about by a medicinal treatment.

Complex and Compound Cures

Compound illnesses have multiple causes. Complex illnesses have single causes with multiple illness consequences. When an illness is complex or compound, multiple cure actions are required. It is necessary to cure each element. Optimal cure sequence can depend on the individual situation. In some cases, the patient might see little relief until the cure progresses significantly or until several causes have been addressed. In other cases, the cure process might consist of a series of improvements. Success with a single element might be misleading, causing the patient and doctor to celebrate prematurely.

Healthiness Causes Cures

Few conventional medical practitioners use the word cure, fewer recommend actions to cure a disease. Alternative practitioners sometimes recommend curing illnesses with health, the best cure.

Improvements in healthiness cure illnesses. Healthy processes cure causal illnesses. Healthy healing cures injury illnesses. Healthy transformations cure attribute illnesses. The healthier the patient, the higher the likelihood and success of a cure.

Compound Illness Example:

- A patient suffering from depression, with unknown causes, might be advised to: improve their diet with healthy food, improve their mind and spirit healthiness with engaging activities and meditation, improve their body with healthy exercise, improve their community interactions through healthy social interactions, and to improve their sleep with healthy sleep. This shotgun technique, addressing many potential causes of illness at once, is often successful. What was the true cause? Once cured, *true cause* loses importance.

Other Cure Concepts

There are many important concepts around the word cure and many misconceptions.

Cure Judgement

Every cure is a judgement, a decision that cause, consequences, the signs and symptoms, are judged to have been addressed. Cured is a positive judgement. Judgements might be wrong, but to cure, we must judge.

Complete Cure

For a single illness element, a complete cure exists when cause and consequences, signs and symptoms, have been addressed. When a complex or compound illness is present, a complete cure exists when all elements of the illness have been cured. A complex cure requires several individual cure elements. A complete cure cures an illness, perhaps a complex or compound illness, not a patient. The patient might have other illnesses which have not yet been cured.

Partial Cure

A partial cure can occur when the cause of an illness is partially addressed. Typically, the patient experiences some relief from effects of the illness. The need for medication might be reduced. Relief from signs and symptoms is not a partial cure unless some cause has been at least partially addressed. It's possible to relieve signs and symptoms as the illness worsens. Addressing signs and symptoms is only a cure when they are causing a secondary illness, and even then, only a temporary cure until the primary illness is cured.

Partial cures are common:

- when a cause in the causal chain of an illness is partially addressed
- with a complex or compound illness, a partial cure exists when some, but not all elements are cured.
- when an injury is partially healed
- when a negative attribute is partially transformed

Complex and compound illnesses are often cured one cure element, one partial cure at a time.

Partial cures are not recognized in current medical practice. It can be difficult to prove a partial cure, because an illness is still present.

Temporary cures

Temporary cures exist when the cause of an illness is temporarily addressed. It can sometimes be difficult to distinguish between a temporary cure, a repeating illness, and a chronic illness. Temporary cures can lead to chronic illness. Although common, temporary cures are not recognized in current medical practice.

A weight loss diet, for example, might be a temporary cure, whereas a permanent change in diet can be a permanent cure. Chronic dieting can lead to chronic illness, seldom to cures. Dietary changes might lead to healthiness and cures, or perhaps to other chronic illnesses.

Conventional medicine tends to view all cures of non-infectious diseases as temporary, as remissions. A failure to understand that an illness is cured when the cause has been addressed. Failure to believe in cures easily leads to failures to cure and supports perceptions of success from treatments that make no attempt to cure.

Maintenance Cures

Many causal illnesses are cured by creating, changing, or removing habits or routines to address a cause. These changes must be maintained to maintain the cure. A healthy diet cures Vitamin C deficiency, but the healthy diet must be maintained. Sometimes, the dietary change is natural, as with infantile scurvy. In other cases, more intentional actions are necessary.

Sometimes an exercise cure transforms the patient, resulting in a permanent cure. Other times, when the cause is an absence of exercise, an exercise cure is a maintenance cure, only persisting as long as the patient continues the exercise.

Illness Cured by Illness

Sometimes an illness cures another illness. There are many ways for this to happen. Many illnesses are a result of a severe imbalance, disharmony, or inability to balance – in body, mind, spirit, or community. Sometimes a new illness moves a balance in a different direction, curing a present illness. Many illnesses cause transformations – sometimes an illness causes a transformation that cures a different illness.

Example:

- A sailor might develop a Vitamin C deficiency working on a ship that provides an unhealthy diet. If the sailor gets sick with a different illness, and they are let off in a port; their diet might be healthed. The second illness cured the deficiency illness. Of course, if the sailor goes back to work on the ship, they will get a new case of Vitamin C deficiency.
- An attribute illness might be cured by an injury that transforms the attribute, producing a cure. This might be a result of a causal illness creating an injury.

Natural Cures, Cured by Health

Many illnesses are naturally cured over time. Our lives change as time passes. Our bodies, minds, spirits, and communities change. Habits and routines change. When a life process changes, even without intention, sometimes without awareness, illness can be cured. Injuries are healed naturally, by natural healing processes. An attribute cause of illness, like a scar that interferes with movement, might fade over time.

The common cold, influenza, and measles are cured when the patient's health addresses the cause. Another cold might arrive, sooner or later. The presence of a new cold does not nullify the cure. The cure was complete - not partial, final - not temporary. Similarly, a patient with an illness caused by a poison might be cured when the source and poison are removed. A new case of poisoning, not a remission, will occur when the cause occurs again.

Alternative Cures

Does a homeopath, a naturopath, a chiropractor, a practitioner of Traditional Chinese Medicine, or Ayurveda, create more or fewer cures, than a conventional doctor? Often, alternative practitioners use the same techniques as conventional doctors, treating signs and symptoms. We often see the word *works*. *"Which medicine, conventional or alternative, works better?"* or *"Do alternative medicines work as well as conventional medicines?"* When it cures, there is no need for debate. It's time to replace *works* with *cures*.

Cured is not defined for most diseases, not for conventional treatments, nor alternative treatments. Debates, even clinical studies measuring differences between conventional and alternative medicines, can often be summarized as nonsense debates posing the nonsense question: *"Which treatment, conventional or alternative,* **does not cure** *better?"* When cure is not the goal, measuring treatment results has little cure importance. For every alternative medicine in the health food store that doesn't cure, there is a conventional medicine in the pharmacy that doesn't cure either. If either could cure, there would be no debate.

A strange truth about medicine today: alternative medicines don't need to cure anything. They continue to sell because patients know that pharmaceutical medicines don't cure the same diseases.

Sometimes a naturopath, or a chiropractor, or another alternative practitioner, sometimes a western medical doctor, spends more time with the patient, listens to the patient, talks to the patient, changes the patient and cures the illness. Producing a real cure that involves the patient, emerges from changes in the actions and inactions of the patient. When a doctor, any type of doctor, even a patient, without the aid of a doctor, aims for a cure, cures are found, although seldom recognized.

Every cure is an alternative. Every illness has a causal chain. Successfully addressing a cause in a causal chain will produce a cure. There are many ways, many alternatives, to address any cause in a chain.

Invisible Cures

All cures are invisible once attained. The illness is gone. Most medical cures are ignored once they occur. A cure is a judgement which cannot be absolutely proven. It's impossible to prove the presence or absence of a cure. Medicines designed to cure are generally marketed as treatments, not as cures. If you cure someone of a non-communicable disease, you are a Saint, or a miracle worker, not a doctor. If you claim to be able to cure, you're obviously insane, or perhaps just stupid, or a quack.

There are no cure statistics.

Spirit Cures

In healthicine, spirits are emotions and intentions, ranging from fear to delight, from despair to hope, from apathy to commitment.

> *Faith does not make things easy, it makes them possible.*
> *Luke 1:37*

Our intentions depend on faith, on what we believe is possible. Faith determines what is possible. Sometimes it determines what happened. When we believe, we can succeed. When we believe we cannot, we easily prove ourselves right. Faith can cause cures. It can also deny them.

Conventional medicine places most faith in not-cures. Faith in the incurability of an illness makes cures impossible. Faith in cures enables cures. But, as Luke advises, faith does not make things easy.

When our doctor's spirits are not aligned with ours, something may need to change before we can find a cure. A patient might say, *"it only hurts when I do this."* The doctor might advise, *"then, don't do that."* The patient can choose to agree, disagree, or find a different doctor.

Spirits are real. Intention is a spirit, a reality, not a placebo. When we believe our illness is curable, but our doctor believes it is incurable, we might be on our own until we find a doctor who believes in a cure. When we cure an illness, our doctor might deny the cure, or more likely, accept the cure, while denying any specific cause of the cure. Medical doctors have little training to understand cures or a cause of a cure.

Sometimes our doctor believes our illness is curable – when we believe it is incurable. Sometimes a patient denies a cure. Cured is a judgement, not a fact. As we practice cure judgements, we will get better at cures.

If you don't believe in miracles,
You could be taking bad advice.
Roy Forbes – Tender Lullaby

Miracle Cures

Do miracle cures exist? The book Miracle Cures: Saints, Pilgrimage, and the Healing Powers of Belief, by Robert A Scott, is an in-depth exploration of the history, and the reality of miracle cures. What did Robert A Scott learn?

Scott does not define miracle cure. He often uses the word *healing* as a cure, even when the cure appears to have been brought about by change to a causal processes or by a transformation. He does have a strong belief that some claims of miracle cures are valid, saying: *"I argue that the faithful feel confident in appealing to the saints for cures because for certain conditions, and under certain circumstances, such appeals actually work."* Scott does not define *cure* nor *works*. However, the book makes it clear that *works* has more meaning than is generally given in conventional medicine – where works often means *"makes the patient or doctor feel better about the disease, but does not cure."*

Scott offers an important caution, with *"I am scarcely the first to point out why a pilgrimage might contribute to a sick person's sense of well being.*

Changes in diet, climate, and daily routine while travelling to pilgrimage shrines might all have beneficial effects together with the powerful experience of being with others with a common purpose." There are many possibilities for non-miracle cures. A pilgrimage can improve healthiness. Improved healthiness can cure.

When thousands make a pilgrimage to a saint or shrine, each changes their diet, their exercise routines, their communities, their environment. Each develops an individual purpose and a common purpose with those on the journey. With so many changes, many cures can be caused by health, by healthy actions. When one person experiences a cure – the story is repeated and magnified over time. We ignore the thousands who failed. The death of a pilgrim is not newsworthy.

We can explain many miracle cures with a basic understanding of the three types of illness and three types of cures. A pilgrimage to a holy shrine affects all three causes and can produce many cures. When someone makes a pilgrimage to a shrine for a cure and finds themselves cured, they are not likely to give credit to their dietary changes, changes to their daily exercise routines, changes to their mental status, their spirits, their sense of purpose. The credit goes to the saint or the shrine. That's why they went on the pilgrimage.

Scott comments on the lack of scientific evidence of cures: *"biomedical and other scientists need to understand that despite the complete absence of independently verifiable, quantitative empirical data about the physical ailments afflicting visitors to medieval shrines....,"* but fails to recognize that many of today's illnesses are mind, spirit, or community illnesses, which do not provide *"independently verifiable quantitative empirical data"* to researchers.

Scott also fails to recognize that there is no science of cure today. He comments about epidemiology, with *"No studies of medieval illness employ modern standards of epidemiology."* Epidemiology studies statistical causes of disease and ignores cure causes. Cure is intentionally not defined in dictionaries of epidemiology. *"Epidemiology is more interested in the prevention and control of disease than secondary and tertiary curative approaches found in traditional medicine."* Thomas C Timmreck, Ph.D. An Introduction to Epidemiology, 2nd Edition.

Can miracles cure? Do miracle cures exist? Every cure is a miracle when we fail to understand causes of illness and associated cures. Today's conventional medicine can easily dismiss every cure claim. The exception proving the rule is infections cured by surgery or poison.

Are Cures Holistic?

What is holistic? Is holism body, mind, and spirit? What about community and environment? Is holism about health? Or about treatments? Or about Cures? *"Holism is a tricky concept...holism is essentially relational;... Indeed what is holistic for one individual is frequently perceived as reductionist by another."* Christopher Lawrence and George Wiesz, Greater than the Parts: Holism in Biomedicine 1920-1950.

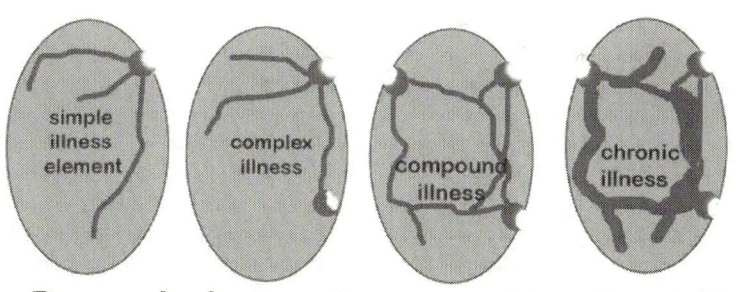

Causal elements are reductionisit
Consequences are holistic
Cures need to be flexible

© Healthicine

Simple illness elements are reductionistic, intentionally reduced to a single cause. They are cured with reductionist techniques. As an illness causes illness, it becomes complex, and more holistic cures are required. A compound illness has multiple causes and requires coordination of multiple cures, a more holistic approach. A chronic illness is more complex and often more ingrained into the patient's lifestyle, requiring more holistic changes to cure. In cures, holism is a scale, not a truth.

Also, each type of cure can be more, or less, holistic:

Process cures: consist of process changes that must be integrated holistically into the life of the patient to produce a cure.

Healing cures: come from health, not from any single action. Health is whole. Healing cures are holistic, creating wholeness where holes were present. They are improved by holistic health improvements.

An attribute cure is a result of a transformation, and thus reductionistic – although its consequences can affect the whole patient.

Life and health are holistic. Causal chains are holistic. Illnesses, even the simplest illness, can produce effects – signs and symptoms throughout the entirety of the patient, from genetics to nutrition, cells, tissues, organs, organ systems, body, mind, spirit and community. We need to use holistic approaches to find the cause, and reductive approaches to produce and judge a cure. Every cure claim is reduced to a judgement, cured or not cured. Every cure has holistic consequences.

Are Treatments Holistic?

Treatments designed solely for signs and symptoms of disease cannot cure. If they cured, we should call them cures. They are not holistic by design, designed to produce specific effects on signs and symptoms, and as a result, often produce *negative effects* on health and healthiness. Treatments have *side effects* or *adverse consequences* because they seldom attempt to improve healthiness. The assumption, in many cases, is that natural healthiness will take over and produce a cure – as with the common cold. In other cases, where medicine cannot cure, treatments come with the suggestion: *"learn to live with the disease."*

Non-Cure Concepts

Although conventional medicine does not define and does not study cures, researchers, practitioners and other skeptics spend a lot of time dismissing and denying cure claims. We generally ignore cure claims. There are no statistics of cures for any disease. We track deaths, but not cure successes.

Medical Treatment

Medical treatments for non-infectious diseases rarely attempt to cure. Diseases are defined and diagnosed without identification of a cause. Most medical treatments are symptomicines. Treatment results are measured statistically. Every cure is an anecdote, so cure result can only be measured anecdotally. Cures are sometimes excluded them from statistical measures.

Symptomicines

Symptomicine products or treatments are designed to address or reduce signs and symptoms of the disease. They can be powerful tools to diminish symptoms and aid the search for a cause. But when used without a cure goal, they allow many illnesses to progress, to grow, to become chronic, and cause other illnesses.

Symptomicine treatments, when successful, intentionally diminish signs and symptoms, which might be confused with a cure.

Without a clear definition and understanding of cured for the condition present – we cannot know if any treatment moves the patient's health towards a cure, or away from a cure, or in some other direction.

Pain lies. Every doctor, every nurse, every physiotherapist knows this. Symptoms lie as well. Symptoms and pain can appear far away from the cause, sometimes far from the damage caused by an illness. Addressing symptoms often falls into the lie.

The Brilliant Function of Pain, by Milton Ward, advises about pain, *"Pain is a guide, not an enemy… Fear of pain, fighting pain, anger at pain, ignoring masking pain will distort your response to pain."* We can extend these concepts to many symptoms of illness.

Preventatives

Is *"prevention the best medicine?"* Is *"prevention is better than cure?"* These phrases are simplistic. Preventatives are not necessarily healthy. Many are speculative, containing significant risk or trading one risk for another – hopefully lesser risk. Preventatives are generally defined by statistical analysis, not by curative analysis.

We can only prevent an illness caused by another illness with a cure. We can prevent chronic illnesses by addressing the chronic cause before it causes any illness.

Few preventatives cure. Health is the best preventative. Cures come from health, not from statistical preventatives.

Perfect Cure

No cure is perfect. When we believe cures must be perfect, we fail to cure and fail to see cures. Cured is a judgement. Life moves forward, never backwards. Many consequences of illness cannot be reversed. Healing is a type of growth. Growth naturally moves forward, not backwards. Attribute cures are a result of changes to physical, mental, spirit or community attributes. Perfection is unlikely.

Cures have long-term, positive and negative effects. We can judge a cure to be present when the cause has been addressed when signs and symptoms have disappeared, and when no more medicines are required. Sometimes an illness leaves damage that cannot be repaired by healing, that can become attributes, sometimes disabilities, to be accepted, not cured. If the damage can be cured, it is are secondary illnesses.

We often think of a cure as a magical event, where all traces of the illness are gone, and health is totally restored. Magical cures are not realistic. We need to accept some permanent consequences of illness, even as we seek cures, even as we cure.

We can adapt the Serenity Prayer to understand cures better: *"give me the strength to **cure illnesses** that can be **cured**, the serenity to accept those that cannot be **cured**, and the wisdom to know the difference."* If we cannot cure it, it might be a disease, but not a curable illness. Every curable illness has the potential to be cured.

Remission vs Cure

Remission is the absence, or diminishing of signs and symptoms, with the continued presence of the cause. Statistically, remissions are often considered to be cures if the patient dies before the disease recurs. Remission of signs and symptoms is not a cure. It often leads to further decreases in healthiness or chronic illness.

Distinguishing between remission of symptoms and cure is easy in theory. A cure exists when a cause has been addressed. Addressing a cause can occur on a scale. Many causes, once they are addressed from the perspective of causing illness, are still present. They are no longer causing illness. Many medical references confuse remission, where the signs and symptoms of illness are hidden, with cure, where the cause has been addressed. Why? In today's conventional medicine, cured is seldom defined and cannot be validated. Claims of remission do not need to be validated. There is no medical test, no scientific test, no definition of remission of a disease, only remission of signs and symptoms. Even placebos can cause remissions.

Statistical Cure

Every cure is a single case, a story, an anecdote. Statistical cures, like cancer cure-rates, are *"presumed to be cured."* There is no evidence that any individual counted in a statistical cure-rate is actually cured.

When we define cured for every illness, we will be in a position to count cures, to create statistics based on cure counts. At present, this is possible for only a few diseases, and not done for any. Once an illness can be cured, cures are ignored.

Placebo Cures

Sometimes when cures occur, especially if the patient has taken an alternative treatment, conventional medical doctors and sometimes other observers, suggest it's *"only a placebo effect."* Placebo effects are a negative judgement about a positive effect. Placebo effects might be blamed even for minor improvements, not just cures.

Placebo effect is in the dictionary, but not placebo cure. Placebos like medical treatments, rarely cure.

It is important to understand that, by definition, placebos do not cause placebo effects. What causes a placebo effect? Let's examine the definition carefully:

Placebo Effect, Webster: *"an improvement in the condition of the patient that occurs in response to a treatment but cannot be considered due to the specific treatment used."* By definition: a paradox. *"in response to a treatment" "but cannot be considered due to the specific treatment."*

Much of what is written about placebo effects is scientific nonsense. The truth about placebo effects is simple. There is no doubt, no disagreement about the beneficial nature of placebo effects. A placebo effect is a real, positive effect. We understand the rest when we study the definition phrase by phrase:

- an improvement in the condition of the patient *(observed by or reported to the physician)*
- that occurs in response to a treatment *(observed by or reported to the physician)*
- *(where the physician does not know the cause of the improvement)*
- but cannot be considered due to the specific treatment used *(according to the physician or medical system)*

What causes a placebo effect? Placebo effects are caused by the physician, by the physician's judgement, when a cause cannot be explained. If we identify the cause, it's no longer a placebo effect, it becomes a real effect, with a real cause.

Every effect, positive or negative, has a cause. The positive effect judged to be a placebo effect might have been caused by the patient's body, by natural healthy healing; by their mind – by changes made in their mind; by changes in their spirits, their community, or their environment. Or it might have been caused by the treatment. When there is no attempt to understand cause much less to study the causal chain, the label placebo effect is a deliberate dead end, a red herring.

It's worse in clinical studies, the so-called scientific gold standard of medicine. In the placebo arm of a clinical study, ALL positive effects might be judged placebo effects. Negative effects? Not. The sum of the *placebo effects* is subtracted from the other side of the study. There is no attempt to understand any single benefit found on the placebo arm of the study. This is commerce, not science.

Placebo effects are scientific nonsense; an excuse to shut down investigation; medical chauvinism based on a belief that only medicines can improve a patient's condition.

We can only claim placebo effect when we do not understand the cause. Every effect has a cause. Every effect has a chain of causes. But placebo effects have no causal chains. When we understand the cause, it's a real effect, with a real cause. When we admit we don't understand the cause, it's a real effect, with a real cause we do not understand.

The attribution of benefits and cures we do not understand to *"the mind"* or to the *"beliefs of the patient"* is usually mystical nonsense, a denial of cause, combined with a failure to study the curative powers of the mind.

It's not hard to understand why conventional medicine often resorts, even embraces, placebo effect explanations. Conventional medicine has little ability to recognize, less ability to address causes stemming the mind, the spirits, or the communities of a patient. Conventional medicine does not recognize any cures that come from placebos. It has little interest in recognizing the effectiveness of alternative treatments, which might force acknowledgment that non-conventional treatments can provide benefits and cures. Placebo effect is a ready excuse, always at hand, seldom questioned, rarely investigated. If investigation finds the cause, it's no longer a placebo effect. But by then, nobody cares.

Regression to the Mean

Another rationalization sometimes used to dismiss positive changes in signs and symptoms, even of cures attributed to alternative treatments is *"regression to the mean."*

Regression to the mean is a statistical observation, not a cause. Actual improvements and actual cures have actual causes. Every instance of improvement or cure attributed to regression to the mean has a real cause.

When an anecdotal cure (every cure is an anecdote), or an improvement in the patient's condition (every improvement has a cause) is attributed to *"regression to the mean,"* it's a nonsense claim, often made with no evidence of a mean. Without a statistical measure of the mean in a group of similar cases, we cannot know if any individual improvement – or any cure - is regressing to the mean, or improving faster than the mean, or moving in the opposite direction of the mean. Regression to the mean is useful to explain statistical results, but not to explain individual results. Every individual change is an anecdote, with a unique, individual story, not a statistic.

Cure Worse Than Disease?

Is the cure worse than the disease? It's a familiar phrase. Francis Bacon actually said, *"The remedy is worse than the disease,"* perhaps in full knowledge that remedies are many while cures are few.

> *To do nothing is also a good remedy.*
> *Hippocrates*

Most remedies are treatments, not cures. Treatments are sometimes worse than the disease, *working* but *not curing*. If they cured, we should call them cures. Treatments present significant risk of adverse effects and risks that the uncured illness will grow in strength with dangerous consequences. Remedies, medicines, and treatments can be dangerous. That's why they require prescriptions. Generally, treatments are not cures. Cures cure.

We fear cures. Curing requires change. Change is risky. Every change, and therefore, every cure, comes with risks. Cures cure illnesses. Sometimes, cures cause illnesses. Sometimes we find a cure to be less desirable than the illness. Health and cures are not trivial.

"Every therapeutic cure, and still more, any awkward attempt to show the patient the truth, tears him from the cradle of his freedom from responsibility and must therefore reckon with the most vehement resistance." Alfred Adler

Every illness can be cured.

The Healthcine Creed

There are no such things as incurable, there are only things for which man has not found a cure. Bernard Baruch

Circles of Illness, Cause, Cure

A causal illness element has a present, active cause: a deficient or excessive, or unharmonious process. An injury illness has a stress cause in the past. An attribute illness element is caused by a deficient or excessive attribute with causes in the past.

The Circle of Illness Elements

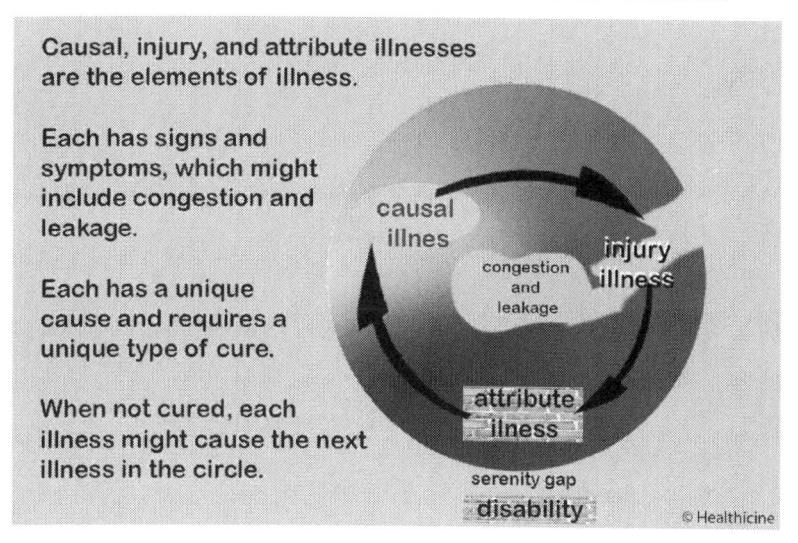

It's useful to view the three types of illness elements in a circle, which can also become a cycle, a downward spiral to unhealthiness, illness, disease, disability, and death. This diagram illustrates the progression of the three elements when not cured.

The Circle of Illness Elements

Causal, injury, and attribute illnesses are the elements of illness.

Each has signs and symptoms, which might include congestion and leakage.

Each has a unique cause and requires a unique type of cure.

When not cured, each illness might cause the next illness in the circle.

causal illnes
injury illness
congestion and leakage
attribute illness
serenity gap
disability
© Healthicine

It is possible for an illness to progress in a different direction, for an attribute illness to cause an injury, or for an injury illness to cause a causal illness – but these are exceptions. The natural flow is for a causal illness – when not cured – to create more damage - to cause injury illnesses. It's natural for an injury illness that cannot be healed to cause a negative attribute, creating an attribute illness. The natural flow of an attribute illness uncured is to cause changes to habits and routines, which can lead to causal illnesses.

Causal illnesses, injuries, and attribute illnesses might cause leakage and congestion in body, mind, spirit, or community.

Injuries and attribute illnesses not cured can lead to disability. The **serenity gap** is the distance between an attribute illness caused by a negative attribute which can be transformed and a disability which cannot be cured, as in the serenity prayer:

> *God grant me the serenity to accept the things I cannot change; courage to change the things I can; and wisdom to know the difference.*
> *- Reinhold Niebuhr*

An attribute illness has the potential to be cured. We cannot cure disabilities. Sometimes an injury cannot be healed. Sometimes the process cause of an illness cannot be addressed. The gap between illness and disability depends on our spirits, our ability to cure, and our belief we can or cannot cure.

The Circle of Causes

We can expand the circle of elements of illness to create a circle of causes. Congestion and leakage can be a cause of illness, not just symptoms. The circle of causes also contains the circle of illnesses. Illnesses can cause many illness.

The Circles of Causes of Illness

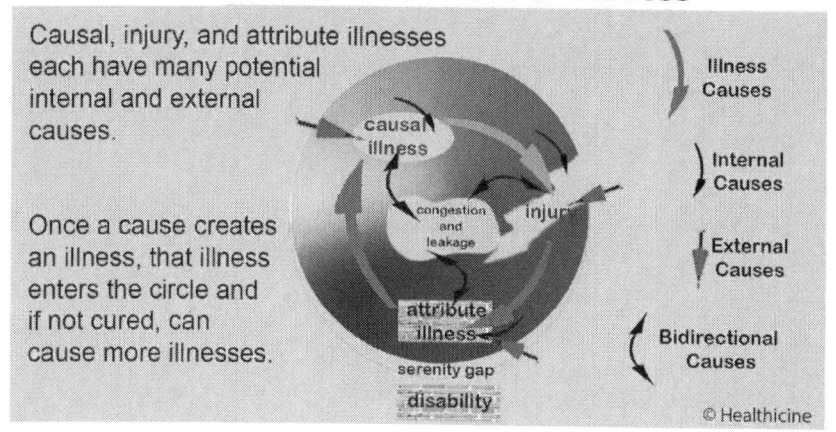

Causal, injury, and attribute illnesses each have many potential internal and external causes.

Once a cause creates an illness, that illness enters the circle and if not cured, can cause more illnesses.

Illness Causes — Internal Causes — External Causes — Bidirectional Causes

causal illness — congestion and leakage — injury — attribute illness — serenity gap — disability

© Healthicine

The circle of causes is full of arrows. Many internal and external processes, forces, and attributes can cause illness.

Every cause is part of a chain of causes. To cure, we focus attention on a specific cause, a cause that cures. For a non-injury illness, there might be many cure causes, each providing multiple opportunities to cure.

The Circle of Cures

The circle of cures reverses the arrows of the circle of illness. The arrows show illness flowing out of the patient. A complex illness with a single cause might consist of a causal illness, resulting in injuries, which lead to an attribute illness, requiring three types of cure actions. We must cure each illness element individually.

Curing causal illnesses is accomplished by addressing a process cause. The causal illness element is cured when the causal chain is broken. Curing of injury illnesses is accomplished naturally by healing. Curing attribute illnesses is accomplished by transformation. Often, transformations cause injuries, and healing is required to complete a transformation. When an illness causes a disability, that cannot be cured. If congestion or leakage occurs, they must be cleared.

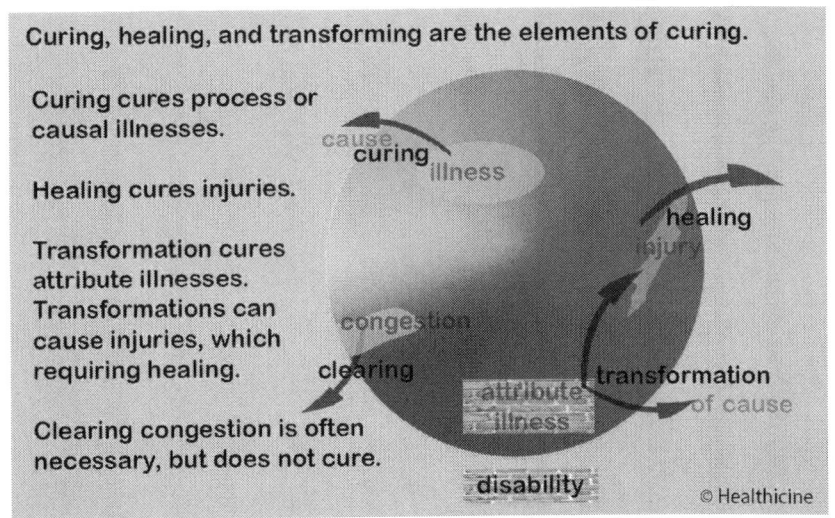

The Elements of Curing

Curing, healing, and transforming are the elements of curing.

Curing cures process or causal illnesses.

Healing cures injuries.

Transformation cures attribute illnesses. Transformations can cause injuries, which requiring healing.

Clearing congestion is often necessary, but does not cure.

[Diagram with labels: cause, curing, illness, healing, injury, congestion, clearing, attribute illness, transformation of cause, disability © Healthicine]

As cures progress, illness elements fade, signs and symptoms of illness fade and disappear. It is sometimes necessary to work on elementary cures in specific sequences. When we fail to cure a prior illness in the circle, a cured illness element can reoccur.

A cure can also cause cures. A transformation cure prompts a healing cure, which might lead to, or facilitate, a causal cure. Sometimes cures lead to illness, sometimes to further cures.

A disease cure often consists of many cure elements, a set of complex and compound illnesses. Every elementary cure is unique to an illness element and the cause to be addressed. Every disease cure is unique to the case. Every cure is an anecdote, a personal story, a personal success. Disease cures are often stories with many parts, a series of anecdotes, which we can only begin to understand as we improve our understanding of cures. Internally caused illnesses are prevented and cured by improving internal healthiness. Externally caused illnesses can be prevented and cured by improving internal or external healthiness, including community and environment healthiness. The best cures come from health, from healthy actions, not from medicines.

Every cure has a cause – we call these causes *"cures."* Every cause is a change.

How to Cure An Illness

Norman Cousins' famous book **Anatomy of an Illness as Perceived by the Patient** is the story of a complex cure, requiring many cure elements. Many doctors find it a fascinating book, but I suspect part of the fascination is the mysterious nature of the cure – which is in no way resolved in the book.

It is important to note that Cousins had a serious illness, but not a disease. He reports that his doctor *"reviewed the reports of many specialists he had called in as consultants. He said there was no agreement on a precise diagnosis."* His condition was serious – one specialist advised that he had one in 500 chance of surviving, that he had never witnessed a recovery from this comprehensive condition.

Perhaps if Cousins had received a diagnosis of a *disease*, it would also have come with a prognosis and a recommended *"treatment that does not cure"*, with advice that he *"learn to live with"* his disease. Cousins might have never cured his illness, might have never written the book.

How did Cousins cure his illness, when the many doctors he consulted could not offer useful advice, much less a cure?

Faith, Belief, Motivation

Norman Cousins believed in himself. He offers a quote from Dr. Schweitzer, *"The witch doctor succeeds for the same reason all the rest of us succeed. Each patient carries his own doctor inside him."* Cousins consulted many doctors, but when none offered a cure, he set out on his own.

Health and Healing

Cousins' actions did not tackle the illness directly. Instead, he worked steadily to improve his health, healthiness, and healing. One of the most effective techniques to cure any illness is to improve healthiness in as many ways as possible, over a long period of time.

Cousins took massive doses of Vitamin C – not as a medicine – as an aid to healing the damage done by the illness, long before Pauling recommended it. He avoided drugs for symptoms, and comments, *"many people tend to regard drugs as though they were automobiles. Each year has to have its new models, and the more powerful the better."*

Cousins advises – and spends an entire chapter on pain, titled *"Pain is Not the Enemy"*. Cousin's learned to laugh with his illness and believes this was a fundamental component of his cure.

Perfect Cure? Miracle Cure?

Cousins does not use the word cure – I suspect if he had, many doctors would have dismissed his story outright. He says, *"Is the recovery a total one? Year by year, the mobility has improved. I have become pain-free, except for one shoulder and my knees, although I have been able to discard the metal braces."* And *"I was sufficiently recovered to go back to my job at the Saturday Review full time again, and this was miracle enough for me."*

Cures are forbidden. *Recovery* is an acceptable claim.

Curing Causal Illness

Cure: *(not defined)* Webster's Medical Dictionary, 3rd Edition
(not defined) The Oxford Concise Medical Dictionary, 9th Edition
(not defined) Barron's Dictionary of Medical Terms, 6th Edition

Many medical dictionaries do not contain an entry for cure. I have not seen a single dictionary definition of cure uses the word *cause*. Medicines can not cure causal illnesses. We must cure them with health.

A causal illness has an active cause, a process, not a thing. A causal illness might be caused by an ongoing deficiency, excess, or disharmony of nutrients, or exercise or rest, or other necessities of body, mind, spirits, community, or environment. Because a causal cure addresses a causal process, it is also a process. A deficiency illness is cured by addressing the deficiency on an ongoing basis. An illness caused by an excess is cured by addressing the excess on an ongoing basis. Illnesses caused by disharmony require understanding to avoid unharmonious actions.

Occasionally, a single cure or cure action cures what is believed to be a causal illness. A repetitive stress illness might be cured with a new chair or a new job. In these cases, the cure re-defines the illness as caused by an attribute – the old chair, or to the process of sitting poorly in the old chair. Hindsight might direct us to causes of illness that seem silly, but no matter – when we find cures.

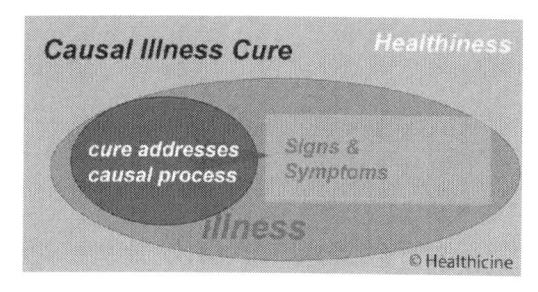

When we address the cause of an illness with a cure action, healthiness grows, and illness fades. Signs and symptoms fade. This might occur slowly or rapidly.

Causal Illness Cured

A causal illness element of body, mind, spirit or community is cured when:

- The causal chain is successfully addressed on an ongoing basis
- Signs and symptoms of illness are no longer present,
- Medicines to treat signs and symptoms are no longer needed.

Proof of Cure: Causal Illness

Conventional medicine today, can cure an illness only if the cause is the growth of an infection by a pathogen, a bacteria, fungus, or another parasite. The infectious agent is transformed to *dead*. When we cure the same illness by improving healthiness, conventional medicine fails to recognize a cure. *"There is no cure for the common cold."*

Once an illness is cured, how can we prove the cause? The cause is no longer present. Sometimes we can bring back the cause to see if the illness occurs again. If not? Maybe we are wrong, but the patient is cured. Exploring a longer causal chain presents more opportunities to cure; however, it can also provide pitfalls, false causes and false cures. When a causal chain splits into two or more independent chains, it presents two independent curable illnesses, such that addressing one chain provides only a partial cure. On the other hand, when a curative action addresses several causal chains at once, it can re-define a compound illness into an illness element, cured by a single action. The complexity of an illness, not just it's perceived complexity, might be resolved by a successful cure or increased by a partial cure.

When a causal illness causes injuries, healing cures are required. When it creates negative attributes, transformation cures are required.

Curing Injury Illness

Cure: *"Heal or make well"* Blakiston's,
"A healing or being healed" Webster's,
"The successful treatment of a disease or wound" Dorland's.

An illness is a hole in health. An injury is a hole in body, mind, spirit, or community. Injuries have causes in the past. A severe stress might come from a process, or an attribute blocking a healthy process. An injury might come from internal forces; a stroke, a pulled muscle, or a hernia, or from external forces; falling down the stairs, a surgical procedure, or a bullet. Injuries can be caused by illness. Many treatments, including many cures, can cause injuries.

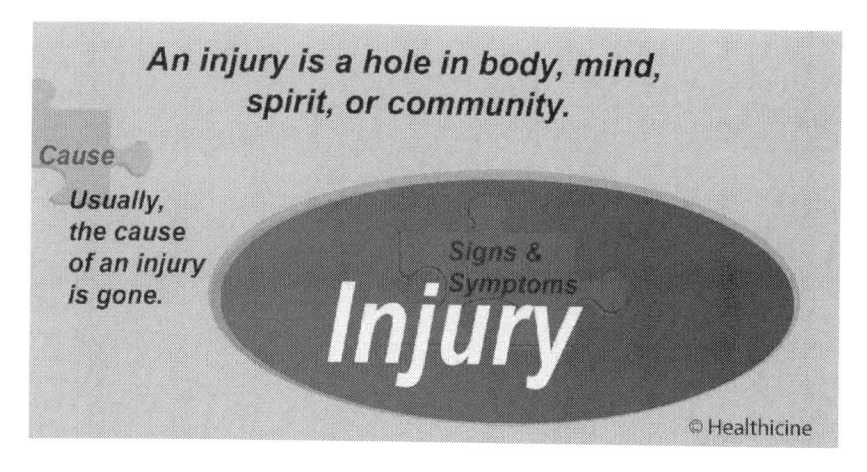

An injury is a hole in body, mind, spirit, or community.

Cause
Usually, the cause of an injury is gone.

Signs & Symptoms

Injury

© Healthicine

Every illness is a judgement. Every injury is a judgement. One person yells *"No Pain, No Gain!"* viewing injuries as a requirement for competition, necessary for improvement. Another might comment, *"I was so stiff and sore it took me days to recover. I'll never do that again."* Some injuries, like arthritis injuries, can be sometimes caused by stress, sometimes by lack of stress. *"Use it or lose it."*

An injury might be caused by a deficiency or an excess of: physical stress - in the body; mental stress - in the mind; emotional stress - of the mind and spirit; spirit stress – the stress of our intentions and goals; or a stress of community. Stress is healthy. Living entities take risks with bodies, minds, spirits, and communities. It's a necessity of life. Life forms that avoid risks are likely to be out-competed or eaten by life forms taking risks and using stress more effectively.

Injuries: Stress vs Healthiness

When healthiness is lower, it's easier for a stress to create injuries. When healthiness is higher, we tolerate more stress and injuries are less severe.

Injuries Occur when Forces or Stresses Overcome Healthiness

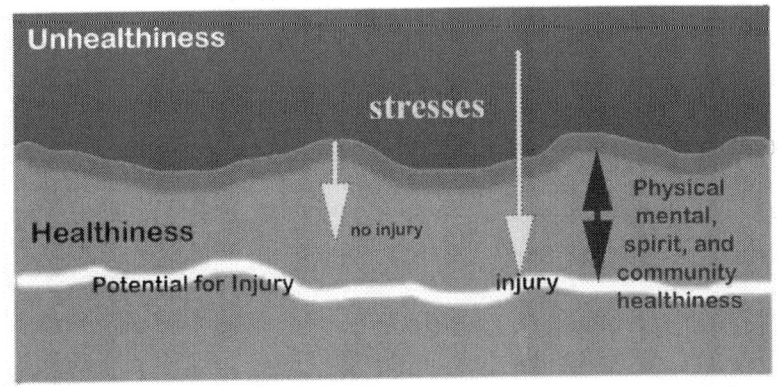

Unhealthiness		
	stresses	
Healthiness	no injury	Physical mental, spirit, and community healthiness
Potential for Injury		injury

© Healthicine

Strength exists separately from healthiness. Too much strength can be unhealthy.

Like any cause of illness, an injury cause has a dual nature. An injury occurs when a stress is too severe for the body, mind, spirit, or community to tolerate. Or, an injury might occur when a specific strength and healthiness of body, mind, spirit, or community is too low, such that a normal or even a healthy stress causes an injury.

A single excessive stress might create several injuries. The concept of an injury illness element is not as critical to curing as with causal or attribute illnesses. The cause is gone. All injuries have the same cure: healing. We might consider a set of injuries, a result of a single cause to be an illness element, although we need to heal several areas. In other cases, we may need to treat a set of injuries as more than one illness, requiring multiple healing processes.

After a causal or attribute illness is cured, it is often necessary to cure injury consequences. Conventional medicine often combines causal illness and injuries into a single disease, searching for a single cure, a more complex cure and fails to see a cure when it occurs. Conventional medicine has no concept of cured for injuries. Cured is a judgement, but there are currently no medical standards for judgement of injuries cured.

Healing

The natural healing force within each of us is the greatest force in getting well.
— Hippocrates

Injuries are cured by healing, by the natural, healthy processes of life. A single cell, the simplest living entity, has repair and healing mechanisms. Tissues are self-repairing due to natural cellular replacement. Wounds are healed. Many injuries to organs and limbs can be repaired by health and healing.

Healing is independent of cause. It does not matter how an arm or spirit was broken – healing proceeds based on the damage, not cause. Healing progresses largely independent of symptoms, independent of treatments, except treatments that aid healing.

Healing proceeds independent of the disease or the illness, often functioning even as the illness is occurring, even when a deficiency or excess of healing causes illness.

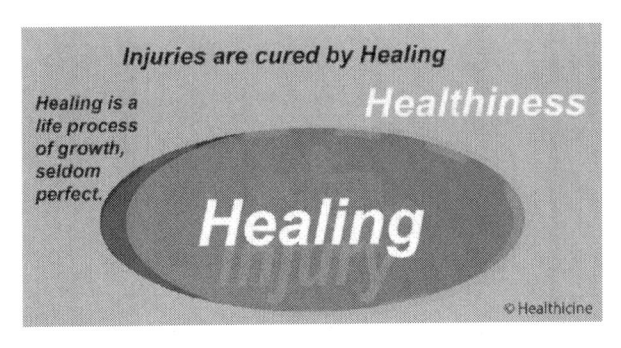

Injuries are cured by Healing
Healing is a life process of growth, seldom perfect.
Healthiness
Healing
© Healthicine

Healing can only move forward, not backwards. Healing masks over the injury, but the repair is seldom perfect.

Perfection is never attainable – cures do not require perfection to be judged cured. We might judge an injury cured when the wound has healed to a scar. We might view a scar as a negative attribute, but it is no longer an injury, no longer the injury illness. As a negative attribute, it might or might not cause an attribute illness, which can only be cured by a transformation.

There are many ways to aid healing cures:

- improving the health of the patient,
- providing rest and resources to allow and assist healing,
- stimulating healing processes, with physical, mental, spirit, and social exercise,
- nutrition,
- medicines to help the body to rest and recover.

Artificially increasing the rate of healing can sometimes help, but might result in growth problems, causing negative attributes.

Injury Cured

An injury illness element of body, mind, spirit, or community is cured when:

- Healing is completed,
- Signs and symptoms of the injury are gone,
- Congestion is cleared, leakage is stopped,
- Medicines for signs and symptoms of injury are no longer needed.

Proof of Cure: Injury Illness

Healing completed is a judgement. Conventional medicine does not judge injuries cured. Injuries are healed, and the word cured is rarely, if ever used in actual practice.

How Medicine Views Injuries

> *The art of medicine consists of amusing the patient while nature cures the disease.*
> *-- Francois Marie Arouet Voltaire*

Conventional medicine excels at physical emergencies, performing best not at healing injuries, but at addressing urgent, dangerous physical conditions. Emergency departments are the busiest place in any hospital. But no emergency clinic can heal. Healing comes from health. Patients are routinely sent home to heal. Of course, a patient with many serious injuries, perhaps a burn patient, will be attended to in detail until they stabilize. Then, those are also sent home to heal. Our bodies, minds, spirits, and communities heal many injuries once the immediate danger has passed.

We pay little attention the efficiency or effectiveness of healing. Sometimes conventional medicine searches for medicines to boost healing unnaturally – if they can be patented. Conventional medicine ignores natural healing. There's no profit in it.

Although injury illnesses can occur in the body, the mind, the spirit, or the community of a life form, today's medical systems only attend to injuries of the body. Injuries to the mind and spirits are often treated as if they were injuries to the body, with drugs that suppress physical symptoms, with no intention to cure.

Healing is dependent on health. Health is slow and steady. Healing takes time. Medical time costs money. It's cost-effective to send patients home to heal. Healing effectiveness is seldom measured.

When the patient has completed healing, there is seldom documentation of a cure. The follow-up, if any, is on the next regular medical checkup. When one patient heals faster, so much the better, when another heals slowly, a physician might note that the patient is healing slowly, rarely making recommendations to optimize healing cures. After all, healing will progress. Medical intervention carries risks. Healthy interventions are not studied medically. Optimal healing is not important in a market-driven, product based, medical system. It can reduce sales and profits. There's little understanding that better healing indicates a healthier patient. There are few, if any, studies of which injuries might benefit from slower healing vs those which benefit from faster healing. Sports doctors often aim for faster healing, even if it reduces overall healthiness, to get a competitor back into the game.

Conventional medicine generally refuses to acknowledge benefits, much less cures, when healing cures are aided by non-conventional medical techniques like chiropractic, Traditional Chinese Medicine, or acupuncture.

Complex Injury Illnesses

Injuries can cause other injuries and illnesses. An injury might induce a change in habits, actions, or movements, resulting in more injuries. An injury might cause a change in diet, sometimes improving healthiness, sometimes leading to additional illnesses. An injury might block a natural flow, causing congestion, which might benefit healing with a scab, or block circulation, causing a failure of healing.

Causal or attribute illnesses can also cause injuries. A common cold might cause a nosebleed. Diabetes uncured causes many injuries. Sometimes the illness that caused an injury is still present, still causing injuries.

When the cause is still present, a complex illness exists, consisting of a causal or attribute illness element, and an injury illness element. A complex illness, consisting of two elements of illness, requires two cures.

When a causal illness persists, healing of injuries provides only a partial or temporary cure.

We can cure many illnesses before they cause injuries. As a causal illness progresses uncured, it can cause injuries, more serious injuries, and other illnesses. Perhaps, as we learn to practice curing, we will cure more illnesses before injuries result. When an illness causes injury, we might view the injury as a failure to notice the illness, failure to address the cause with health, failure to cure before injuries occur.

Compound Injury Illnesses

Sometimes, life sucks. Sometimes, we injure ourselves, and then we are injured again and again – for no related reason. Healing of multiple injuries occurs independently, but healing takes energy. Each individual injury can take longer to heal when multiple injuries are present.

Curing Attribute Illness

Cure: *"To remedy or eradicate,"* Funk and Wagnalls Canadian College Dictionary, 1989.

Sometimes we cure an attribute illness by transforming or removing an attribute, sometimes by creating or adding a missing attribute.

Most Attributes are Healthy

Life entities use attributes in the natural processes of living. Normally, they do not cause any illness. When an attribute causes a large drop in healthiness, illness can occur.

Attributes can be Positive, Neutral, or Negative

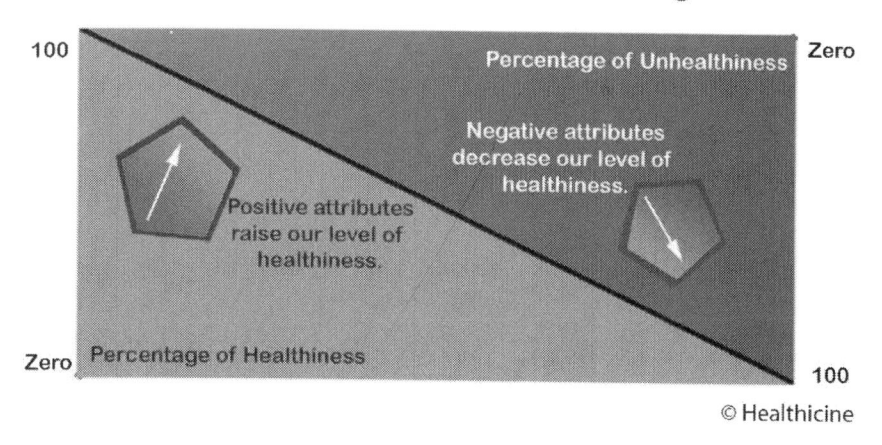

© Healthicine

An attribute illness, like every illness, is a negative judgement. It exists when the signs and symptoms of illness are judged to be caused by a negative attribute. It can be difficult to determine if any attribute is truly positive or negative, healthy or unhealthy. A positive or neutral attribute of body, mind, spirit, community or environment might become negative over time, or in specific situations.

In some cases, the judgement of a negative attribute is clear. In others, an attribute might be viewed beneficial by some, negative by others, or beneficial sometimes, negative at other times. Pessimism and optimism are healthy attributes in moderation, unhealthy in excess.

Attribute: Boundary Illnesses

The most common attribute illnesses are boundary illnesses. A boundary can be a fact, a physical, mental, spirit or community reality, sometimes an imaginary thing, a mindset, an attitude, or belief, or a law, separating inside from outside, separating good from bad. Healthy living entities use boundaries to let health factors enter, to keep unhealthy factors from entering, and also keep healthy factors inside while allowing unhealthy factors to escape or to be excreted.

The smallest life entity, a single cell, has a cellular membrane separating inside from outside. The cell must constantly maintain the health of the membrane. If it weakens or malfunctions, the cell can grow ill and die. Humans have many physical, mental, spirit, and community boundaries which must be maintained, and sometimes destroyed, to maintain healthiness. Boundaries are never perfect. Life is about living, not perfection.

We often use boundaries as preventatives. Life forms also use boundaries as tools. Boundaries can be physical, like skin, or a door; mental, like attention and rules; emotional attributes like confidence and fear; or spirit attributes – like drive or boredom. An unhealthy boundary might be a result of our imagination, of faulty beliefs, but its effects are real, not imaginary and the resulting illness is real. Unhealthy boundaries might exist for long periods without causing illness, sometimes hardly noticed until we challenge ourselves in a new way. We compensate for unhealthiness naturally, healthily.

There are two common types of boundary failures; each has two sides.

Blockages can fail to allow the good to enter, or the bad to exit. **Leakages** can allow negative factors to enter or healthiness to escape.

Mental blockages might be transformed by understanding, or by correcting invalid perceptions or ideas. A spirit blockage can diminish intent, motivation, and passion, which can lead to feeling *"I'm bored,"* to depression, or possibly suicide. In other circumstances, boredom might be a motivator. A community blockage, a rule or law against a healthy activity, can decrease healthiness, causing illness. Blockages can be caused by growth. Healing, seldom perfect, often leaves blockages in body, mind, spirit, or communities.

Leakages are the other common boundary illness, leaking healthiness or allowing unhealthiness to enter. Leakage attribute illnesses of the physical body include minor bruises and wounds, but most leakages are subtle, ranging from faulty digestion and elimination of waste to leakage of attention and memories. Mental leakages can occur when we are distracted and forget what we need or need to attend. They occur when incorrect or negative facts intrude and become part of our belief systems, allowing truth to be mistaken or to leak out. It's not easy to be certain which facts, memories, calculations, or plans are correct. What was true yesterday might not be true today. When we become disoriented in our mental state, to the point where we cannot remember the day, or what to do in the morning, the afternoon, or the evening, we are suffering from a severe mental leakage, which might be an illness – or if incurable, a disability. Spirit leakage can cause us to lose motivation, intention, faith in ourselves, or allow harmful motivations and intentions to enter.

Humans live in communities. We continually create and maintain healthy boundaries in our communities. Leakage of self, in a community, can lead to one type of attribute illness, blockage or isolation to another.

Unhealthy boundary attributes often have causal chains in the past. We cannot go back in time to address a cause. The present cause, the attribute, is not active. It's a thing, not a process. However, sometimes the cause of an unhealthy boundary is a present causal process, which also must be addressed to maintain a cure.

Cause of a Negative Attribute

Finding and addressing causes of attribute illnesses can be useful to prevent future attribute causes – seldom useful to cure. Negative attributes can be caused by faulty growth (cataracts, cleft lip, hernia, learning, etc.), by injuries, or by faulty healing of injuries (callouses, scar tissue, relationship scars, or failures). They might also be a result of an ongoing causal process.

We often think of illness as having an external cause. This valuable concept provides many cures. Negative attributes often have causes external to the living entity, while the attribute, the cause of a present illness, is part of the living entity or their lifestyle.

Negative mind and spirit attributes might be caused by unhealthy mental processes, or unhealthy motivations or intentions. They might even be a result of success – when a success is due to an unhealthy activity. Medical practice does not distinguish causes, or illnesses, of the mind, spirit, and community. Is PTSD a blockage of the brain, the mind, the spirits, of the afflicted – or all three in some cases? Are criminal activities, where the criminal is judged to be insane, a negative attribute of the brain, or the mind, or the spirits, or the community? I am certain we can find examples of each. Conventional medicine treats physical, mental, and spirit illnesses with medicines – as if they are all founded in the chemical composition of the body. We often treat community illnesses with prisons, as if the individual must be punished, as opposed to curing the community. Negative community attributes might be caused by an individual or by something in the community's past, even fear of something in the future. Where can the cause of an illness be found? Only in a cure.

Negative attributes can also be caused by natural imperfections in, or natural consequences of the processes of life, growth, living, and ageing.

> *You don't fall ill, you slide. Sometimes very slowly, over a long period of abuse and lack of awareness.*
> --- Thérèse Bertherat, Carol Bernstein

Attribute causes often creep or slide into existence, slowly growing as time passes, invisible until an illness progresses to a crisis, or until a person undertakes a new or infrequent activity. Sometimes a minor attribute illness, hardly noticed, causes another attribute illness, and another until we perceive a problem. Finding a cure often requires a thorough analysis. Use of symptomicines allows illness elements to persist and grow unobserved.

Negative attributes can cause injury. Acne blockages can cause infections. High blood pressure can lead to aneurysms. The presence of a physical scar can disrupt movement, resulting in accidents. Blockages and leakages of mind, spirits, or community can result in severe illnesses, including mass murder – which our current systems treat as crimes, not as symptoms of illness.

Transforming: Curing Attribute Illnesses

Attribute illness elements are cured by transforming: releasing, repairing, removing, or changing the negative attribute. When a missing attribute causes the illness, the cure is to create or add the missing attribute. The term used in this text is transformation. Health is a verb. Transformations health negative attributes. Once a negative attribute is transformed to be neutral or positive, additional cure processes may be necessary; clearing congestion and healing damage caused by the illness and by the transformation.

There are many types of transformation. Curative transformations might occur in the body, the mind, the spirits, or communities – depending on the attribute. Transformations can cure many leakages of body, mind, spirits, and community. Each attribute cause has many potential curative transformations.

We judge an illness cured by a transformation to be an attribute illness. Dentists transform teeth; priests transform spirits; counsellors transform relationships, grandparents transform perception. Many illnesses which cannot be cured by simple healing; cannot be cured by addressing a process cause, are cured by a transformation of cause.

Healers and alternative practitioners sometimes speak of the transformation of the patient. Only the attribute causing the illness element needs to be transformed.

Attribute Illness Cured

An attribute illness element of body, mind, spirit, or community is cured by transformation of the cause to a neutral or healthy state. Transformation of a negative attribute often results in injuries requiring healing to complete the cure.

An attribute illness element is cured when:

- The attribute cause has been transformed to a non-negative state,
- Healing of injuries caused by the illness and by the transformation has completed,
- Signs and symptoms of the illness are no longer present,
- Medicines for signs and symptoms are no longer needed.

Proof of Cure: Attribute Illness

Conventional medicine has no concept of an attribute illness. At present, cured is only defined for an attribute illness when the attribute is an infection cured by surgery. Surgery is often an attribute cure, from extracting a sliver or an ingrown toenail to complex procedures like a heart transplant. There are no medical tests for cured, in these cases.

How can we be certain an attribute illness is cured? When an attribute is changed, we cannot go back to the previous state. We cannot undo a surgery to test if it was the cure. Transformations move forward. Sometimes, we can reverse the attribute change to see if a new illness occurs. If we cured myopia with glasses, we can easily remove the glasses to see the illness again, because the eyes were not actually transformed. However, if we cure myopia with eye exercises – proof of cure is much more difficult. Every individual cure is an anecdote. Anecdotal cures don't contain sufficient proof for bureaucratic, statistics-based medicine.

Some negative attributes are of the mind, the spirit, or the community. An illness caused by a negative attribute of mind or spirit might be cured by transformation of belief or intention. A patient might consult a doctor about a worrisome illness, a new bump or blemish on their skin. The doctor might explain it to be a mole or other natural feature, curing the illness with knowledge. When a patient *sees the light,* understands and accepts a perceived illness as normal, even healthy, an illness has been cured. Beliefs that cures come only from medicines limit our understanding, limit cure successes.

A psychologist, friend, parent, priest, mentor, even an enemy might cause a transformation of mind, of memories, beliefs, or spirits, motivations and intentions. Conventional medicine does not recognize these actions as curing, does not recognize these results as cures even when a disease disappears. Instead, it's viewed as a remission of signs and symptoms.

It's sometimes important to understand the cause of the negative attribute. If the cause of the attribute is still present, it might recreate the attribute, leading to a new case of the illness. Sometimes, the attribute cause is a result of another illness or a result of a chain of illnesses which must be addressed to maintain a cured state.

Conventional medicine ignores cures of attribute illnesses. Surgery is sometimes recognized as a cure, but there is rarely a test of cured. We view cures as magical. They must be perfect. Transformation to perfection is impossible. So, attribute cures become impossible.

We use attributes extensively for prevention of illnesses, in building codes, manufacturing codes, food processing codes, labelling standards. But conventional medicine does not have a concept of an attribute cure, even when it cures by transforming an attribute.

Rudyard Kipling wrote:

> *The cure for this ill is not to sit still,*
> *Or frowst with a book by the fire;*
> *But to take a large hoe and a shovel also,*
> *And dig till you gently perspire;*
> *And then you will find that the sun and the wind,*
> *And the Djinn of the Garden too,*
> *Have lifted the hump -- The horrible hump --*
> *The hump that is black and blue!*

This is an attribute cure, the work in the garden released and transformed the "horrible hump" and facilitated a natural healing clearance.

Illness, Injury, or Disability?

The distinction between an injury and an attribute illness might be difficult to discern. There is a simple technique. To cure an attribute illness, the negative attribute must be transformed. If it can be healed, it is an injury illness – healing is also a transformation. Sometimes the distinction is determined by the success of a cure. Attribute transformation techniques like surgery and leakage repair techniques like stitches and bandages can also be useful in curing injuries, helping them to heal.

Three Elements of Illness

causal illness / injury illness / attribute illness

© Healthicine

When we look at any element of illness, we find gradations and overlap between causal illness elements, injury illness elements, and attribute illness elements.

How can we be certain which classification is correct?

Only by curing.

If addressing a process cause cures, it was a causal illness. If making the patient's life processes healthier cures the illness, a healthy cure, it was a causal illness – caused by the patient's lack of healthiness. When healing cures, it was an injury illness. When transformational cures succeed, it was an attribute illness.

Examples:

- Shin Splints is a causal illness, cured by addressing the process cause.
- A broken leg is an injury illness, cured by healing.

- A missing limb is a disability, incurable, or possibly cured by a prosthetic, by adding an attribute.

Every illness is a judgement. An attribute illness, a handicap, and a disability have similar features. Handicaps and disabilities entail issues outside of the issue of cure – beyond the scope of this book. By definition, every curable illness has the potential to be cured. If a disability is cured, it was an illness. If it is healed, it was an injury illness. When an illness is judged to be incurable, it might be judged a disability, a handicap, or perhaps simply a natural feature.

Cures are defined by success. Success is defined by cures. Treatments that do not cure can sometimes shift our perception around the circle, suggesting other ways to cure, but only when we aim to cure.

Confusing Healing and Transformation

Both conventional and alternative medicine discriminate poorly between transformation and healing. Many books with the word cure in the title claim to be about healing. Few use the word cure in their contents. Most are about transformations, not about healing. It's easy to be confused. Transformations that cure attribute illnesses often cause injuries, which require healing to complete the cure. When we see references to cures that heal, if the author is using the word heal correctly, the illnesses being cured are injuries. However, medical writers often use the word *healing* for *transformations*.

Every cure is a story, an anecdote. Health and healing are slow and steady. Healing cures seldom make interesting stories. Stories of transformations followed by healing are interesting, increasing publicity and common confusion.

Healing is a type of transformation, but not every transformation is a type of healing.

Curing Chronic Illness

Any illness is chronic when the cause is chronic. Chronic is an attribute of cause. All chronic illnesses are attribute illnesses, cured by transforming the chronic nature of the cause. A chronic infection is a causal illness with a chronic cause. Chronic injury illnesses have chronic stress causes. Attribute illnesses are chronic by nature until their causes are transformed.

We might view the cause of a chronic illness as a meta-cause. When a cause persists over time, the persistent nature of the cause is a higher-level cause, a chronic attribute. Chronic bacterial infections are chronic illnesses caused, not by bacteria, but by the chronic presence of dangerous bacteria or by a chronic level of unhealthiness allowing normally healthy bacteria to invade, grow, and create infections.

In most cases, a single occurrence of a chronic causal process or injury stress is insufficient to cause illness. The chronic nature of an illness becomes clear only after an extended period. Obesity is a chronic illness, but the cited cause, over-eating, does not cause obesity until it becomes chronic. People who are obese are often told to go on a diet. A diet cannot cure a chronic disease unless it transforms the chronic cause. Sometimes the chronic nature of an illness is cured by a habit, which replaces an unhealthy habit or routine, transforming process cause. Chronic dietary deficiencies might cause chronic physical, mental, or spirit illnesses.

When a stress is chronic, it can create a chronic illness. In many cases, the chronic stress that causes an illness is healthy when not chronic. Repetitive stress injuries are chronic illnesses, caused by the chronic attribute of a stress.

In each case, the cure is to address not the cause, but the chronic attribute of the cause. There are no magical cures for chronic illnesses. However, sometimes they disappear mysteriously, when the life of the patient or their environment changes, without the conscious intention of the patient or doctor. We can easily miss these cures. An unintentional cure seldom gets attention.

We cure chronic illnesses with health, by improving the health of the patient, their communities or environment. Health is slow and steady. Transformations, slow or rapid, must be lasting to cure.

Chronic diseases often require multiple cures because they can easily accumulate causes when not cured.

Curing Chronic Causal Illnesses

Addressing the chronic nature of a chronic causal illness requires identification of a chronic attribute of the cause. A chronic cold is not caused by the bacteria, but by the chronic unhealthiness of the patient or their environment.

Curing Chronic Injuries

When the cause of an injury is persistent, there exists a chronic injury illness. Each specific case might be an injury illness. The sequence of injuries is a meta-illness, a chronic illness. Often each individual injury is too small to be judged as an illness. These illnesses are sometimes called repetitive stress injuries, repetitive strain injuries, or work-related disorders.

A secretary might develop carpal tunnel syndrome from excessive stress or bad posture. Attempts to cure the illness without addressing the chronic cause are doomed to failure. The way the worker sits might be a chronic process cause, which can be changed by changing the work processes. However, there are two cures required, the change of a chair, and healing of the injuries. Healing of injury illnesses often requires rest and time.

Curing Chronic Attribute Illnesses

Attribute illnesses are naturally chronic, persisting until the attribute cause is transformed.

Chronic Stress

We can view every illness element as caused by stress and cured by addressing the stress. A chronic illness element is caused by a chronic stress, by the chronic attribute of a stress. Life makes healthy use of stress. As a result, stresses can easily accumulate. Accumulated stress can create compound illnesses requiring multiple cures. It can also create chronic illnesses caused by the stress of stress.

Stress can take over the mind and depress the spirits. Stresses on body, mind, spirits, and community are similar, in many ways, to pain. Pain lies. Stress can lie, distracting our attention. When we focus on our pain, we might magnify it, making it unbearable. We magnify with attention, with anxiety. We sometimes dismiss stress by paying no mind – which might be useful or incorrect action depending on specific circumstances. Stress, like pain, can be real, or imaginary.

When we stress about our stresses, we increase them, creating stress-stress. Stress-stress is chronic. When it causes an attribute illness, the cure is a transformation of our obsession.

Stress-stress is sometimes learned. We can learn to magnify our stress, without realizing we are doing so. Stress can also be taught. Marketers sell anxiety: are your teeth whiter than white? Do you need X? Ask your doctor about Y?

Stress-stress can also be unlearned. We can learn techniques to minimize the stress, to cure chronic illnesses caused by the stress of stress. Focussing on simple tasks like breathing, reduces stress, by taking our attention away from the stress.

Today, we rarely treat chronic stress illnesses with intentions to cure. Cured is not defined for diseases caused by chronic stress on body, mind, spirit, or community. Instead, we buy medicines to diminish symptoms and suck it up as the levels of stress rise higher, until something breaks, forcing us to cut back.

Chronic Illness Cured

A chronic illness element is cured when:

- The chronic attribute of the physical, mental, spirit, or community cause has been addressed,
- If an underlying illness is the cause, it must also be cured,
- Healing is completed,
- Signs and symptoms are no longer present,
- Medicines to treat the signs and symptoms are no longer needed.

Sometimes a chronic illness presents two illnesses which must be cured, one a direct result of the cause and another a result of the chronic nature of the cause.

Proof of Cure: Chronic Illness

Conventional medicine currently views chronic illnesses as incurable. As a result, little attention is paid to cures when they occur. In current practices of conventional medicine, there is no proof of cured for any chronic illness.

We cannot prove obesity cured by over-eating only once or twice to see if it returns. It will only return as a result of chronic over-eating. A return to chronic over-eating will produce signs and symptoms of additional weight long before obesity occurs again. Many chronic illnesses creep slowly providing ample evidence of cause.

When we cure a chronic illness by adding something, we can sometimes test the cure by removing the new attribute. If chronic conditions were cured by adding a habit, like a daily walk or a resolution to maintain a positive attitude, we might easily reverse the new change to see the consequences.

In some cases, there is danger in testing the cure. Many chronic illnesses create disabilities and testing a cure risks additional disability.

Judgements: Illness, Cause, Cure

> *"You cannot see the wind,*
> *you can only see that there is wind."*
> G.K. Chesterton

When we cure an illness, by addressing the cause, the illness disappears. Was it really there? We could not see the illness. We could not touch it. We can't see that it is gone. We might see the cause. We see the consequences, signs and symptoms, but symptoms lie. We often refer to the signs and symptoms as the illness. But this can distract us from cures. An illness is not a thing; it is an intersection of cause and consequences, a judgement that an illness is present. Signs and symptoms are a consequence of the cause, not the illness itself.

Illness: A Judgement

An illness is a negative health condition with a cause. Negative is a judgement. Every health condition, positive or negative, is a judgement. One person might perceive an illness, another not. A doctor, or a friend, might notice an illness the patient ignores or denies. A patient might fuss and fret over an illness denied by the doctor.

Diagnosis of a case of disease is a judgement by a medical professional, but still a judgement. Diagnoses are sometimes incorrect, or incorrect in the estimate of severity.

Cause: A Judgement

Every cause is a judgement. We are never certain something was the cause of an illness in a specific case. We can only exercise our best judgement, learn from experience. Doctors are exposed to more experiences and opportunities to learn. But today, conventional doctors are encouraged to ignore cures, to ignore specific causes.

Clinical studies base judgement on statistics, which provide stronger general knowledge while blurring and ignoring information from individual cases. Every cause, every illness, and every cure is an individual case, not a statistic.

Cure, Curable, Cured: Judgements

Every cure is a judgement. A curable illness is a negative condition in a living entity; an intersection of cause and negative consequences, which we believe, or judge can be cured. Cured is a judgement.

How can we be certain an illness has been cured? How can we know if the treatment action caused the cure? We know a diagnosis is a judgement. We trust our doctor's judgement or seek a second opinion. Unfortunately, according to current published research, many doctors refuse to make judgements of cured. We should not be surprised. Cured is seldom medically defined. Doctors are not trained to diagnose cured. Conventional medicine has no techniques, and no training to diagnose cured for most medical conditions.

Incurable: A Judgement

Can an illness be incurable? Incurable is a judgement made in a specific case, which cannot be proven. We can decide to accept a disability, handicap, or another attribute as cannot be cured. Later we might change our mind. A cure can falsify any claim of incurable.

When a condition is judged incurable, it is no longer a curable illness. The judgement has changed its status.

When we claim an illness is curable – the claim might be proven by a cure, but it cannot be falsified. We might give up attempting to cure, which does not prove it incurable. Barron's Dictionary of Medical Terms does not define cure, but it defines incurable as *"being such that a **cure** is impossible within the realm of known medical practice."* Cure and incurable are currently defined only with reference to medical treatments.

Judgements: Individuals and Communities

Judgements can be made by a patient, by their family, friends, or neighbours. There might be agreement about a judgement or not. Judgements by a professional have higher value – but professionals can also disagree. At present, all cure judgements are ignored by conventional and most alternative medical communities. If we wish to cure – we are often on our own, like Norman Cousins.

Truth?

Can we find truths? What is the source of truth? Whether we look historically, or recently, at science, or the media, we can learn that truth comes not from any reality, but from individuals and from communities.

We each live our lives in many communities. Our lives are constantly changing. Our communities are constantly changing.

We must make our own judgements, being prepared to listen to other people's judgments, and prepared to change our truths and judgements.

We must each find our own truths about our illnesses, causes, and cures.

Proof of Cured

Today's conventional medicine offers no proof of cured, ignores most cases of cured. Few cures can be proven or disproven, due to the absences of a definition of cured.

How can we be certain an illness has been cured? Proof is a scale, not a binary reality. Often, individual proof is sufficient. My cold is cured. The cure needs no validation. Proof is stronger when our communities agree and when more respected communities agree, it grows even stronger. Legal communities provide judgements and proof in law. Unfortunately, for most diseases, medical communities provide no proof of cure. There is seldom any medical difference between remission and cure.

What if it comes back?

An illness is not a thing that can go away and come back. When we have successfully addressed the cause, and healing completed, the illness is cured. If the cause returns, a new illness will occur. We must treat recurrences as new cases, as a return of the cause, not return of the illness if we wish to understand cures.

Cures come from Health

Health is honest and true. All cures come from health. We often try to trick a disease. We cannot trick health. Illness is caused by a lack of healthiness, cured by improving healthiness.

Causal cures are healthy cures, improving healthy life processes of the patient. Many causal illnesses are cured by health, naturally, sometimes before we become conscious of them. Sometimes a life process changes, without intention, without awareness, mysteriously curing an illness.

Only healing can cure an injury. Healing is part of growth, always active, even when no illness is present, facilitated and aided by healthiness, by proper diet, by physical, mental, spirit, and community exercise, rest, healthiness, and support. The immune system is also a healing system, a powerful curing system.

Transformation is change. We often fear change, and rightfully so. Change moves us forward in life. Change can cure. But change can also cause illness. Transformations that cure are healthy, but many curative transformations also produce injuries and pain, and require healing.

Every illness is a consequence of a decrease in healthiness and causes further decreases in healthiness. Healthy change is the best cure. Healthiness is the best preventative. The cure for any illness is an improvement in health, a specific kind of healthiness for each type of illness. When we raise healthiness, we reduce unhealthiness, and illnesses are cured.

How many diseases are best cured by health? When we make cures our goal, all of them. Even incurable conditions are often best treated with healthiness.

We need to spend time, energy, and money pursuing cures, searching for healthier cures, less time pursuing treatments, patents, and profits, with no intention to cure.

At present, **health care** is a euphemism for ***dieae-care***. No health clinic cares for us when we are healthy. Illness, curable illnesses, might be present long before a specific disease is diagnosed. But no insurance will pay for treatments without a diagnosis of disease. What insurance will pay for the best cure, when the best cure is not a medicine, but an improvement in healthiness? Insurance companies pay for medical treatments not for health improvements. Will insurance pay for the best preventative? Not unless it is on the list of insurable treatments. They will not pay for cures either – unless they are on the list. With insurance, results do not count. Bureaucracies rule by rules, not by results.

We can visualize the concepts of illnesses and cures in this diagram:

A Calculus of Curing

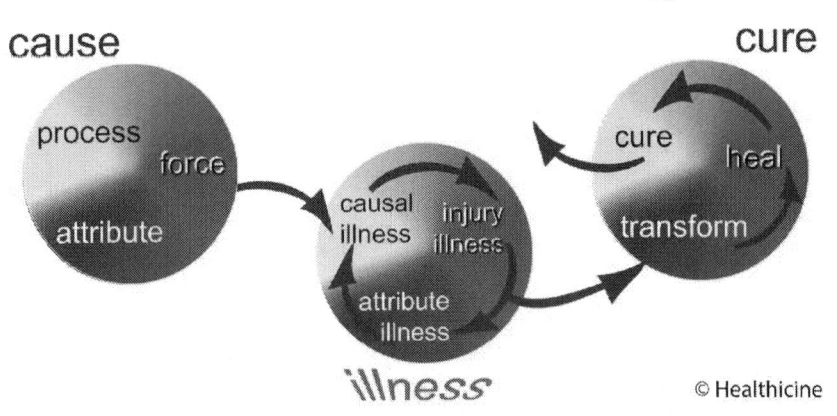

cause — process, force, attribute

illness — causal illness, injury illness, attribute illness

cure — cure, heal, transform

© Healthicine

Every illness has a cause. Every cause is either a process cause (an active process or absence of process over time), a force cause (excessive stress or absence of stress) or an attribute cause (a something or absence of something). These three types of causes produce three distinct types of illnesses, respectively: causal illnesses, injury illnesses, and attribute illnesses. We cure each types of illness with a different cure action, respectively: causal cures (curing), healing cures (healing), and transformational cures (transforming).

A causal chain results in a single element of illness. When the cause is repeating, it causes a repeating illness. When the cause is chronic, it causes a chronic illness. Repeating and chronic are attributes of a cause.

Only a specific illness can be cured, in a specific patient, one illness element at a time. Every patient is unique, with unique causal chains of illness. Every illness is unique. Every cure is unique, sometimes even for the same disease in the same patient at a later time in their life. We can study, learn, and understand similarities to find cures, but each cure is a unique success story, an anecdote.

As we study elements of illness, elements of cause, chains of cause, the repeating and chronic nature of causes, and the elements of curing, we will learn to take simple diseases apart, and cure them, in many cases with health, not medicines. We will learn useful truths about curable illnesses, incurable conditions, and come to understand the fundamental difference between an illness and a chronic illness.

We can begin with simple illness elements and simple cures, progress to higher understanding, developing techniques to encompass more complex illnesses and diseases, more complex cures.

It's time for a science of medicine, time for a science of cures.

> *"We have not succeeded in answering all our problems—indeed we sometimes feel we have not completely answered any of them. The answers we have found have only served to raise a whole set of new questions. In some ways we feel that we are as confused as ever, but we think we are confused on a higher level and about more important things."*
> The Workshop Way of Learning - Earl C. Kelley

We will not begin to succeed until we begin to cure. To find cures, we must define cured for every illness element, build scientific definitions of cured for each case of a disease.

To learn to cure, we must practice curing. Many current treatments are distractions, ignorant of cures. We need to learn that cures for many diseases cannot be found in medicines, nor in alternative medicines. Cures come from health.

We need to move beyond *the cure,* beyond the naive belief that every illness, every disease has one best treatment. We need to move forward through many cures, to search for better cures. Every illness has many opportunities to cure. Each cure has strengths and weaknesses. Some cures are better for some patients in specific cases. Other cures might be better for other patients, or at other times. Some cures are faster, some more reliable, some more effective. To find the best cure for each case, we need to move away from the bureaucracies of conventional medicine. Until we accept the possibility of many cures for any illness, we cannot begin to explore the many dimensions of curing.

> *Every illness can be cured. The Healthicine Creed*

In the final analysis, we will learn we cannot change our illnesses without changing ourselves, because illness is a part of our lives, part of our healthiness. We cure by changing our lives, our health, our bodies, minds, spirits, communities, and environments. We cure by becoming healthier.

Appendix: A Cure Flowchart

The following flow diagram can be used as a guide to cure any curable illness by curing one illness element at a time and gathering more understanding about the causes of illness as the cure progresses.

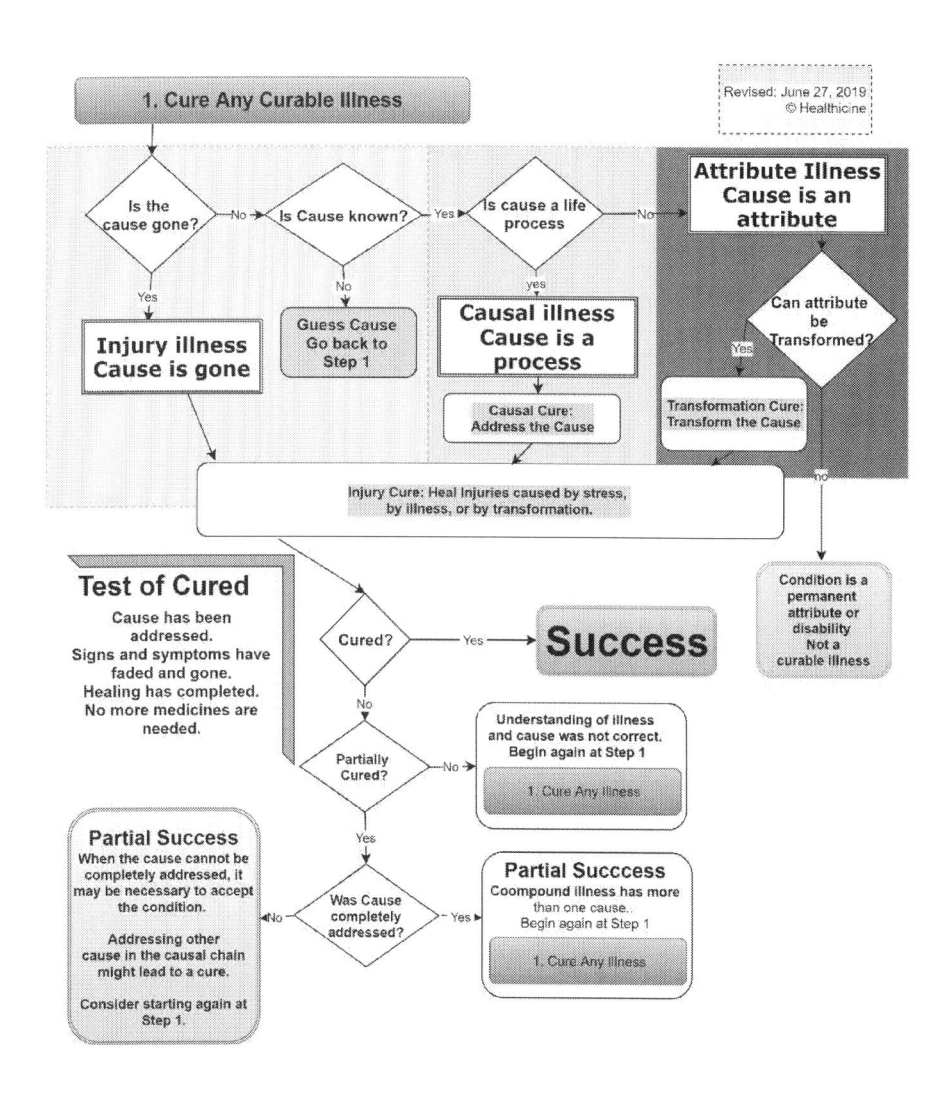

Made in the USA
Middletown, DE
30 July 2019